Open Source Software

Making Business Applications accessible

Els **Van Vossel**

Fabien **Pinckaers**

An OpenSource Solution to Financial and Analytic Accounting

Record Entries Quickly, Customize Financial Reports and Manage Budgets

Open Object Press

Open Source Software
Making Business Applications accessible to All Companies

Ope*ERP

An OpenSource Solution to Financial and Analytic Accounting

Record Entries Quickly, Customize Financial reports and Manage Budgets

by Els Van Vossel and Fabien Pinckaers

First Edition

Many of the designations used by manufacturers and suppliers to distinguish their products are claimed as trademarks. Where those designations appear in this book, and Open Object Press was aware of a trademark claim, the designations have been printed in initial capitals.

While every precaution has been taken in the preparation of this book, the publisher and the authors assume no responsibility for errors or omissions, or for damages resulting from the use of the information contained herein.

Open Object Press

Open Object Press is a division of **OpenERP S.A.** (www.openerp.com)

Copyright © 2011 Els Van Vossel and Fabien Pinckaers

First edition July 2011   **ISBN :** 978-2-9600876-2-8

Open Object Press

40, Chaussée de Namur
1367 Grand-Rosière
http://openerp.com/

Special Thanks to Marc Laporte, Olivier Laurent et Gary Malherbe

Open Object Press

40, Chaussée de Namur
1367 Grand-Rosière
http://openerp.com/

From the same Editor

OpenERP for Retail and Industrial Management – Steps towards Sales, Logistics and Manufacturing Integration, 2009, Fabien Pinckaers and Geoff Gardiner, ISBN: 978-2-9600876-0-4

Drive your Sales & Marketing Activities with OpenERP – Close Leads, Automate Marketing Campaigns and Get Accurate Forecasts , 2011, Els Van Vossel and Fabien Pinckaers, ISBN: 978-2-9600876-1-1

Streamline your Manufacturing Processes with OpenERP – A Simple Approach to Manage the Manufacturing and Supply Chain Complexity, 2011, Els Van Vossel and Fabien Pinckaers, ISBN: 978-2-9600876-3-5

The Authors: Els Van Vossel and Fabien Pinckaers

Contents

The OpenERP Solution   xi

I   Use OpenERP Online   3

II   Initial Configuration of Your Instance   5

III   Customer Invoicing & Payments   9

1   **Simple Customer Receipts**   11

2   **Invoice your Customers**   13

3   **Keep Track of your Customer's Payments**   15

4   **Get your Money in**   19
    4.1   Financial Analysis of Partners 19
    4.2   Multi-step Reminders 22

5   **Analyse your Turnover**   25

IV   Accounting Management   27

6   **Advanced Invoice Management**   31
    6.1   Creating a Customer Invoice 31
    6.2   Tax Management 38
    6.3   Cancelling an Invoice 39
    6.4   Controlling a Supplier Invoice 40
    6.5   Credit Notes / Refunds 43
    6.6   Advanced Setup: Payment Terms and Fiscal Positions 43

7 Advanced Cash Management   47

    7.1 Managing Bank Statements 47

    7.2 Cash Register Management 49

    7.3 Miscellaneous Operations 50

8 Recording Journal Items   53

    8.1 Recording Sales Entries through Journal Items 53

    8.2 Miscellaneous Operations: Creating an Opening Entry 54

    8.3 Journal Entries 55

    8.4 Manual Reconciliation Process 55

    8.5 Productivity Tips 59

9 Automate your Payments   63

    9.1 Supplier Payments 63

    9.2 Automatic Reconciliation 66

V Analytic Accounts   69

10 To Each Enterprise its own Analytic Chart of Accounts   71

    10.1 Case 1: Industrial Manufacturing Enterprise 71

    10.2 Case 2: Law Firm 73

    10.3 Case 3: IT Services Company 75

11 Analytic Entries   79

    11.1 Integrated with General Accounting 79

    11.2 Manual Entries 79

    11.3 Automated Entries 80

    11.4 Analytic Models 81

VI Financial Analysis   83

12 General Ledger and Trial Balance   85

13 Balance Sheet and Profit & Loss Report   87

14 The Accounting Journals   **89**

15 Tax Declaration   **91**

16 Management Indicators   **93**

17 Good Management Budgeting   **95**

18 The Accounting Dashboard   **99**

19 Analytic Analysis   **101**

    19.1 The Cost Ledger 101

    19.2 Inverted Analytic Balance 101

    19.3 The Cost Ledger (Quantities Only) 102

    19.4 Analytic Balance 103

    19.5 Analytic Journals 103

    19.6 Analytic Entries Analysis 104

VII   An Introduction to Multicurrency Principles   **105**

20 Getting Started with Multicurrency   **107**

    20.1 Receivable Account in Currency 107

    20.2 Bank Account in Currency 108

21 Creating an Invoice in CHF   **111**

    21.1 Defining a Receivable Account for CHF 111

    21.2 Creating the Invoice 111

22 Encoding Payments   **113**

    22.1 Paying an Advance 113

    22.2 Reporting and Follow-ups 113

    22.3 Customer Pays the Remaining Amount 114

    22.4 Write-off and Exchange Rate 115

VIII   Managing your Assets   117

23 Depreciation Methods   119

24 Asset Categories   121

25 Registering Assets   123

26 Analysis of Assets   125

IX   Configuring Accounts from A to Z   127

27 Periods and Financial Years   129

   27.1 Defining a Period or a Financial Year 129

   27.2 Closing a Period 130

28 Managing your Tax Structure   131

29 Chart of Accounts   137

   29.1 Using a Preconfigured Chart of Accounts 137

   29.2 Creating a Chart of Accounts 138

   29.3 Virtual Charts of Accounts 141

30 Journals   143

   30.1 Configuring a Journal 143

   30.2 Controls and Tips for Data Entry 144

31 Payment Terms   147

32 Opening and Closing a Financial Year   149

   32.1 Steps to Open a New Financial Year in an Existing OpenERP Configuration 149

   32.2 Generating the Opening Entry 150

   32.3 Closing a Financial Year 151

33 Steps to Start your Financial Year   153

34 Putting Analytic Accounts in Place   155

34.1 Setting up the Chart of Accounts 155

34.2 Creating Journals 157

34.3 Working with Analytic Defaults 158

About the authors 159

    Fabien Pinckaers 159

    Els Van Vossel 159

Index   **1**

The OpenERP Solution

OpenERP can build a new breed of business applications, more modular, more customer-friendly, fully web-based, which others cannot due to the heritage of their legacy systems.

OpenERP is a comprehensive suite of business applications including Sales, CRM, Project management, Warehouse management, Manufacturing, Financial management, and Human Resources, just to name a few. More than 1000 OpenERP modules are available from the OpenERP Apps market place (http://apps.openerp.com/).

The key to continued business success is effective and integrated Accounting & Financial Management, and that is precisely the main topic of the book you are reading. OpenERP's Accounting features are flexible and highly developed to assist you in managing all aspects of financial management.

OpenERP offers you integration with your sales & purchase cycle, so that invoices can easily be generated for the accountant's review according to various criteria. This way, the accountant can skip most of the encoding and dedicate himself to Financial Analysis and Reporting. OpenERP's management dashboards and extensive Analysis reporting allows the financial staff to keep a clear view on Customers and Suppliers, as well as on the company's financial status.

OpenERP's Accounting is totally integrated into all of the company's functions, whether it is general, analytic or budgetary accounting. OpenERP's accounting function is double-entry and supports multiple companies, as well as multiple currencies and languages. Moreover, the application offers a lot of accounting features to both accountants and non-accountants.

Accounting that is integrated throughout all of the company's processes greatly simplifies the work of entering accounting data, because most of the entries are generated automatically while other documents are being processed. You can avoid entering data twice in OpenERP, which is commonly a source of errors and delays.

So OpenERP's accounting is not just for financial reporting – it is also the anchor-point for many of the company's management processes. To learn more about accounting integration with other business applications of OpenERP, we refer to our books about Logistics Management, Manufacturing and CRM.

Integration with other business applications also heavily reduces the manual encoding of supplier and customer invoices, because they can be generated automatically from purchase and sales orders.

The specific and easy-to-use *Invoicing* system in OpenERP allows you to keep track of your accounting, even when you are not an accountant. It provides an easy way to follow up your suppliers and customers. You could use this simplified accounting when your (external) account keeps your books, but you would like to keep track of payments. No accounting knowledge is required!

Of course, OpenERP also allows accountants to do their job in a flexible, convenient way. Through Journal Items, entries can be recorded quickly, because the system will automatically propose counterpart accounts.

OpenERP provides integrated analytical accounting, which enables management by business activity or project and provides very detailed levels of analysis. You can control your operations according to actual management needs, rather than based on the charts of accounts that generally meet only statutory requirements.

OpenERP now also allows you to keep track of your Cash Moves through the new OpenERP Cash Box, which allows you to enter incoming and outgoing cash transactions. The balance of your cash box will even be checked against the number of coins in it!

Asset management through predefined depreciation rules, directly from the invoice: a great way to keep track of your investments. Asset entries can automatically be posted in the corresponding journal and according to the accounts specified. Analyse your assets by grouping and filtering relevant data in various ways. Of course, with the Asset Management application you can depreciate according to the pro rata temporis rules.

Budgets can be managed in OpenERP as well, both on general accounts and analytic accounts. You can define your own budgetary positions to tell the system for which accounts you want to keep a budget, giving you the freedom to keep budgets on any kind of account. Associated graphs and budget reporting allow you to get a good view on what is to come.

Multi-currency principles in OpenERP will be described in a dedicated chapter. Invoice your customers in various currencies and clearly distinguish between exchange rate differences and write-off entries.

OpenERP is an impressive software system, being easy to use and yet providing great benefits in helping you manage your company. It is easy to install under both Windows and Linux compared with other enterprise-scale systems, and offers unmatched functionality. Whether you want to test OpenERP or put it into full production, you have at least two possible starting points:

- you can use OpenERP Online by subscribing to http://www.openerp.com/online/;

- you can install the solution on your own computers to test it in your company's system environment.

In this chapter, the easy-to-use *OpenERP Online* solution will be briefly explained. For more information about installing OpenERP on your computer, please refer to the on line documentation.

 Some Interesting Websites from OpenERP

- Main Site: http://www.openerp.com,

- OpenERP Online Site: http://www.openerp.com/online,

- Online demo at http://demo.openerp.com,

- Documentation site: http://doc.openerp.com,

- Modules and Extra Features: http://apps.openerp.com,

- Community discussion forum where you can often receive assistance: http://www.openerp.com/forum.

Part I

Use OpenERP Online

Nothing is easier for you to discover OpenERP than subscribing to the OpenERP Online offer. You just need a web browser to get started.

The Online service can be particularly useful to small companies, that just want to get going quickly at low cost. You have immediate access to OpenERP's Integrated Management System built on the type of enterprise architecture used in many organizations.

OpenERP's Online offer includes several services: hosting at high bandwidth, database management, stable security update, backups, maintenance (24/7 server monitoring), bug fixing and migrations.

OpenERP guarantees that the software running on OpenERP Online is exactly the same as the Open Source official version of OpenERP. Any improvement made on OpenERP will be available online. This allows you to easily switch from the online version to the local version anytime.

So even if the OpenERP Online solution might be the best solution to suit your needs today, you can easily switch to an installation on your own servers according to your company's changing requirements or growth. You are also able to change your service provider anytime, while continuing to use the exact same system. Hence, you do not depend on your host. In addition, OpenERP works with standard and open formats and programming languages which allow you to export your data and use them in any other software.

These advantages give you total control over your data, your software, your platform.

If you want to start working with the online platform, you can navigate to http://www.openerp.com/online or click the Subscribe & Start button from http://www.openerp.com. After successful registration, you will be able to configure and use OpenERP online. To log in to your OpenERP Online account, you will receive a username and password. You can build the software to fit your needs, at your own pace!

OpenERP Online - Software as a Service - is hosted by OpenERP and paid in the form of a monthly subscription. The pricing model is extremely simple. OpenERP charges a fixed fee per month per user. You will get an invoice each month according to the number of users registered in the system at that time. If you add new users during the next 30 days, they will only be charged with the next invoice. You can find the details of current pricing and payment options at http://www.openerp.com/online.

Free Trial

For a month's free trial, check out OpenERP's http://www.openerp.com/online, which enables you to get started quickly without incurring costs for integration or for buying computer systems. After the free trial expires, you can easily continue using OpenERP Online.

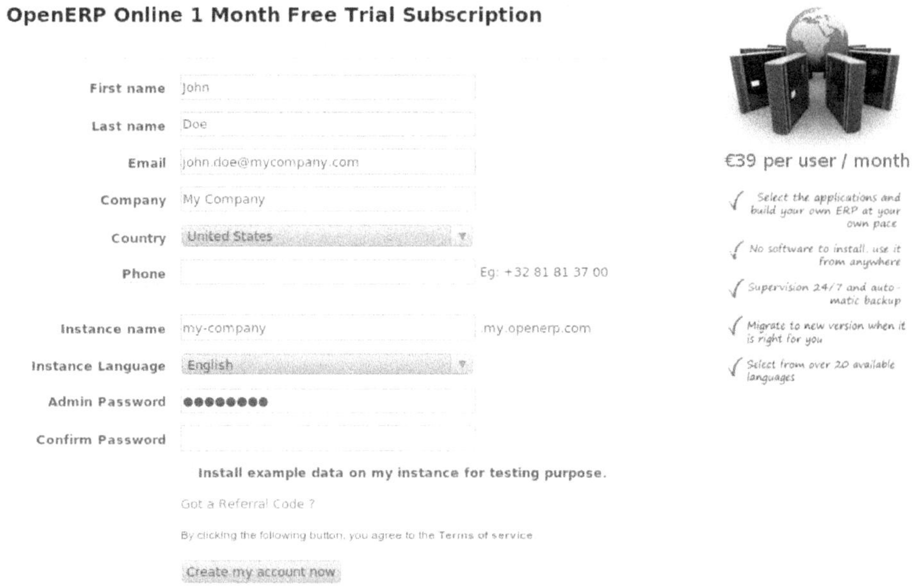

OpenERP Online 1 Month Free Trial Subscription

First name	John
Last name	Doe
Email	john.doe@mycompany.com
Company	My Company
Country	United States ▼
Phone	Eg: +32 81 81 37 00
Instance name	my-company .my.openerp.com
Instance Language	English ▼
Admin Password	●●●●●●●●
Confirm Password	

Install example data on my instance for testing purpose.

Got a Referral Code ?

By clicking the following button, you agree to the Terms of service

Create my account now

€39 per user / month

✓ Select the applications and build your own ERP at your own pace

✓ No software to install, use it from anywhere

✓ Supervision 24/7 and automatic backup

✓ Migrate to new version when it is right for you

✓ Select from over 20 available languages

Figure 1: *Subscribe and Start with OpenERP Online*

Part II

Initial Configuration of Your Instance

If you want to focus on your customers, you need tools: to capture all the knowledge you have available; to help you analyse what you know; to make it easy to use all of that knowledge and analysis. OpenERP invites you to discover the Accounting & Financial Management Business Application!

In this chapter, you can start exploring OpenERP!

Use a web browser of your choice to connect to OpenERP Web.

Figure 2: *Welcome Page*

At first, the welcome page will allow you to install the Business Applications you need. For more information about other business applications than `Accounting & Financial Management`, we refer to the existing books available from the OpenERP website (http://www.openerp.com, `Buy` tab).

To install an easy system to keep track of your accounting, click the `Install` button below the icon *Invoicing*. To install *Financial Management*, click the `Install` button below the icon *Accounting and Finance*.

Change from Invoicing to Financial Management

By changing the access rights of a user, you can easily switch from Invoicing (access rights Invoicing & Payments) to Accounting and Finance (access rights Accountant or Manager).

For this quick start we will install `Invoicing`.

OpenERP suggests that you configure your database using a series of questions. In the software, these series of questions are managed through so-called `Configuration Wizards`.

Select the `Chart of Accounts` if you want to install a predefined chart of accounts. You can select from a list of localised charts of accounts. Select for instance the `Belgium - Plan Comptable Minimum Normalise` chart. Click `Configure` to install the selected chart of accounts.

Now OpenERP will show you the home page with two buttons, i.e. *Accounting* and *Settings*. Click the `Settings` button to check your configuration. In this dashboard, you can also see a progress bar indicating the elements you already configured.

Figure 3: *Settings Home Page*

Click the option `Set Company Header and Footer` to indicate what should be printed in the company header and footer of your reports. You can enter address data for your company, create your bank accounts, and much more. When you are finished configuring the company header and footer, you can return to the `Settings` dashboard by clicking the *Settings* button at the top of the screen. Now simply check the box in front of this option to indicate that the company header and footer have been completed.

In case you want to add extra features, such as **Sales and Purchase Management**, click `Install Applications` from the *Settings* dashboard to enrich your software with more business applications.

You can also decide about your default user preferences, such as what will your user interface look like, will the screens only show the most important fields - `Simplified` - or also fields for the more advanced users, the `Extended` view. You can also define your user language and time zone (very convenient when scheduling meetings). By default, OpenERP will display interesting and helpful tips when you open a screen (option which can be unchecked). As soon as you finish this wizard, the system will automatically check the box, to indicate that configuration is completed.

User Preferences

You can easily switch from `Simplified` to `Extended` view by changing your *User Preferences* (the *Preferences* button next to the *Home* button).

Not every company calls its customers "Customers", so there is a configuration option which lets you choose different labels for customers (and suppliers, according to the business applications installed). Click the option `Use another word to say Customer` if you want to change this. As soon as you finish this wizard, the system will automatically check the box, to indicate that configuration is completed.

You can easily create more users with the `Create Additional Users` option if needed.

From the `Accounting` part, you can configure your company's bank accounts, review your accounts and journals, as well as your payment terms.

By configuring your company's bank accounts, you can have the software automatically create a bank journal for you. Select the bank account type, type the account number and the Bank Name, and when you save the entry, your Bank Journal will automatically be created with the Bank Name and the Account Number. The general ledger account for this bank will also be created for you.

Simplified or Extended view

In Simplified view, you will not see the bank journal. Switch to Extended view first.

When you click the Review your Financial Journals option in the Accounting part, you will notice that OpenERP will propose basic journals, such as purchase, sales and miscellaneous journals. You can easily change them and add new journals according to your needs.

OpenERP also comes with some standard payment terms, allowing you to start really quickly.

You will see the progress bar move as you check configuration options.

OpenERP's modularity enables you to install a single Business Application (such as *Accounting*) if that is all you need. Of course, you can choose to also install Sales Management, for instance, to handle quotations, sales orders and sales invoices as well.

Reconfigure

Keep in mind that you can change or reconfigure the system any time through the *Add More Features* option in the main toolbar.

When you choose a business application for installation, OpenERP will automatically propose to add or configure related (smaller) applications to enrich your system.

Part III

Customer Invoicing & Payments

OpenERP provides various features to keep track of your invoicing and payments. The simple workflow of invoicing, with efficient encoding of the payment process of your customers, makes OpenERP more adoptable. In this section, we discuss two processes, the easy workflow for non-accountants who just want to keep track of their payments, and the complete accounting section. Note that only the customer process will be described, but of course OpenERP offers equal invoicing and payment methods for suppliers. In OpenERP, the invoicing workflow is very simple. You can see it in the following figure:

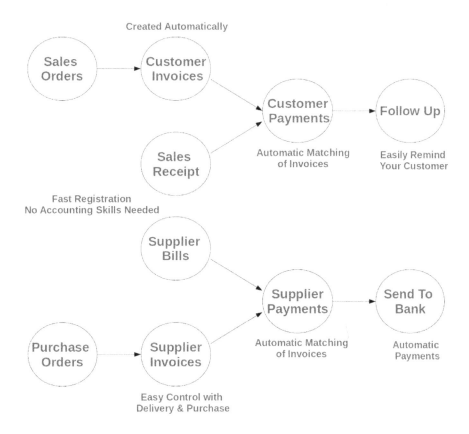

Figure 4: *Invoicing Workflow*

An invoice can be generated from various documents, such as a *Sales Order* and a *Purchase Order*, or at the time of confirming a shipment. These methods will be proposed when you use OpenERP as a truely integrated system.

Of course, companies often work together with an external accountant who keeps their books. In that case, you would like to know which invoices exist and have been paid.

The specific and easy-to-use *Invoicing* system in OpenERP allows you to keep track of your accounting, even when you are not an accountant. It provides an easy way to follow up your suppliers and customers. You could use this simplified accounting in case you work with an (external) account to keep your books, and you still want to keep track of payments. The `Invoicing` system includes receipts and vouchers (an easy way to keep track of sales and purchases). It also offers you an easy method to register payments, without you having to encode complete abstracts of account.

Simple Customer Receipts 1

When you sell products to a customer, you can give him a true invoice or a *Sales Receipt*, which is also called *Customer Receipt*. Sales Receipts are merely a kind of sales ticket and not a real invoice.

When the sales receipt is confirmed, OpenERP creates journal items automatically and you can record the customer payment related to this sales receipt. The easy invoicing system does not require extensive accounting setup, so you will be up and running quickly!

You can create and modify a sales receipt from the menu *Accounting → Customers → Sales Receipt*.

Figure 1.1: *Defining a Customer Receipt*

 Extended View

To display Sales and Purchase Receipts in the Customers / Suppliers menu, you need to use the `Extended` view. The view can be changed with the user `Preferences` button next to the `Home` button in the main toolbar.

When you create a new *Sales Receipt*, you have to enter the *Customer* for whom you want to create a voucher. You can also define *Sales Lines* in the *Sales Information* tab. Here you have to define *Account*, *Amount* and *Description*. At the bottom of the form, you will have two options for *Payment*: one is *Pay Directly* and another is *Pay Later or Group Funds*. When you select the *Pay Directly* option, you have to enter the bank *Account*. The *Total* amount displays automatically with calculation of tax (if you select VAT to be added) when you click the *Compute Tax* button.

When you purchase products from a supplier, you will receive a *Purchase Receipt* (a ticket), which is also called *Notes Payable* in accounting terminology. When a purchase receipt is confirmed, it creates journal items automatically and you can record the supplier payment related to this purchase receipt, just like for the sales receipts.

You can create and modify the purchase receipt through the menu *Accounting → Suppliers → Purchase Receipt*.

The *Purchase Receipt* form looks like the *Sales Receipt* form. In this form, carefully select the journal.

Figure 1.2: *Purchase Receipt*

Invoice your Customers

It is surprising to see that in the 21st century, most companies still process quotations & invoices manually, mostly by post or email. The trend is clearly for personal communication to disregard these legacy media, and replace them with instant messaging, social networks, etc. The *Electronic Data Interchange* (EDI) platform is here to try and open OpenERP to more modern communication systems, where electronic documents are exchanged and synchronised between business partners in real-time.

Initially, OpenERP will support a simple EDI mechanism for certain OpenERP documents, such as Sales Orders, Purchase Orders and Invoices.

Indeed, the integrated email and invoicing system in OpenERP allows you to create an invoice and automatically send an email with the invoice link to the customer.

The customer then has several options. If your customer also has an OpenERP instance, he can easily import the invoice you have sent him, simply by clicking the link.

Below, you find an example of such an EDI flow:

1. Your company issues a Sales Order, a Purchase Order or an Invoice for a specific partner, let's say Camptocamp.

2. Partner Camptocamp receives an email with a link to an online preview of the document.

3. In the online preview of the document, Camptocamp can read the document, download or print the PDF version, and then choose between a couple of options:

   1. import this document in his own OpenERP instance, simply by providing the instance address;

   2. ask to create a new OpenERP online instance, where the document will be pre-imported;

   3. ask for the raw EDI document, which the partner can then import in his own third-party software through a corresponding EDI import system.

4. Partner Camptocamp can also choose to directly pay online through Paypal or any other mechanism provided by your company.

The email notification is freely customisable as an Email Template from the *Settings → Configuration → Email → Templates*.

To get the EDI and automatic emailing of orders and invoices to work, you need the `EDI` module, which is installed by default. You need to add an email adress to the partner and make sure the "Opt-out" checkbox is not selected. Ask your system administrator to configure an Outgoing Mail Server. Note that email notifications will be added to a mail queue and processed once in a while, but you can force emails to be send directly from the *Settings → Email → Messages*.

The email your customer will receive, will look like the image displayed.

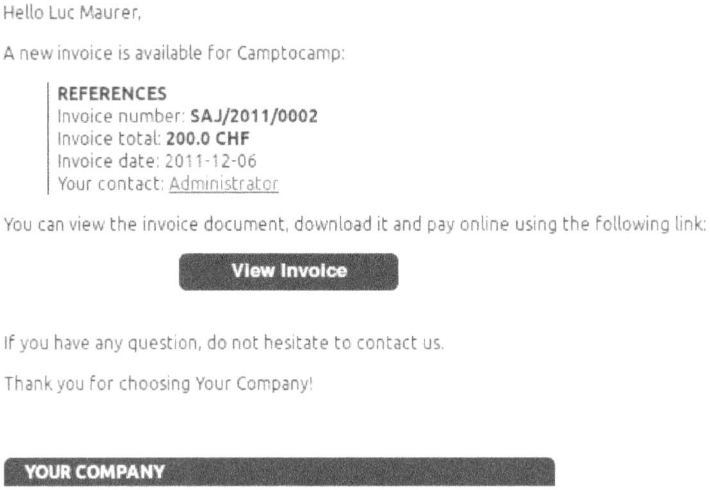

Hello Luc Maurer,

A new invoice is available for Camptocamp:

> **REFERENCES**
> Invoice number: **SAJ/2011/0002**
> Invoice total: **200.0 CHF**
> Invoice date: 2011-12-06
> Your contact: Administrator

You can view the invoice document, download it and pay online using the following link:

View Invoice

If you have any question, do not hesitate to contact us.

Thank you for choosing Your Company!

YOUR COMPANY

Figure 2.1: *Mail to Your Customer*

Keep Track of your Customer's Payments 3

It is important to efficiently keep track of payments of your customers and suppliers. People who have no accounting knowledge and just want to use OpenERP to keep an eye on their payments, can set the `Invoicing & Payments` access rights from the `User` form.

Customer Payment allows you to register the payments you receive from your customers. In order to record a payment, you have to enter the customer, the payment method (= the journal) and the payment amount. OpenERP will automatically propose the reconciliation of this payment with any open invoices or sales receipts, credit notes and (advance) payments.

You can register Customer payments in OpenERP from the menu *Accounting → Customers → Customer Payment*; click *New* to register a payment.

Figure 3.1: *Customer Payment*

Suppose you have an invoice of 3000 EUR; the amount you actually receive from the customer is 2995 EUR. You would consider the invoice as entirely paid. How would you proceed?

To create a new *Customer Payment*, select the customer, key in the *Paid Amount*, e.g. 2995 and select the *Payment Method*, i.e. your bank journal. Any open invoices, credit notes or advances for this partner will be displayed on the `Payment Information` tab. In this example, the 3000 EUR invoice will be proposed.

Now you have to tell OpenERP that you want to consider the invoice as fully paid. Simply click the invoice line on the `Payment Information` tab to make it editable. Now select the *Full Reconcile* checkbox, and notice that the amount changes to the full amount of the invoice.

Select the proper option in the `Payment Difference` field, i.e. *Reconcile Payment* (you would use the *Keep Open* option if you want to claim the 5 EUR from the customer). The write-off amount is already proposed automatically, but you have to enter the *Counterpart Account* so that write-off entries

Figure 3.2: *Fully Pay*

can be generated by OpenERP. You can also enter a comment about the reconciliation (by default, Write-Off will be proposed). Then post your payment.

Analytic Accounts

When you do analytic bookkeeping as well, you can enter an analytic account for the write-off too.

This easy payment system also allows you to post a payment that you cannot directly attribute to a customer as an advance.

Let us take the following example. A customer has two open invoices, one of 2000, one of 1500. He pays 1000, but you cannot assign this to any of the two invoices directly. You can just enter this payment as an advance. How do you proceed?

When you key in an `Amount paid` of 1000 in your *Customer Payment*, the amount will be attributed to the oldest invoice. You do not want this, because you have no idea yet of what invoice the amount should be linked to. Click the amount in the first line and set it to 0. Validate the payment. The system will now create an advance payment of 1000 for the customer concerned.

Supplier Payment

The `Supplier Payment` form allows you to track the payment to your suppliers in the same way as a customer payment.

From the menu *Accounting → Suppliers → Supplier Payment*, click the *New* button to create a new *Supplier Payment*.

Another way of keeping track of your payments is the way accountants will do it, by encoding `Bank Statements`. For more information about this, please refer to the chapter on *Advanced Invoice Management* (page 31).

You can also push your accounting further by importing your payments electronically through a CODA file you receive from the bank. To do this install the `account_coda` module.

How should you proceed?

You have to enter your company's bank account(s) for which you want to accept CODA files. Go to the menu *Accounting → Configuration → Financial Accounting → Accounts → Setup your Bank Accounts*. Choose the bank account type you want to use (IBAN or normal bank account). For electronic payments, you should use IBAN; do not forget to also enter your bank's BIC code.

Figure 3.3: *Supplier Payment Form*

Bank Journal

When you save the bank account through the Setup your Bank Accounts wizard, a bank journal will be automatically created for that account.

Then add the bank account details for each partner that will pay you through a bank. You can do this in the Partner form, on the `Accounting` tab.

Download the CODA file from your bank to any directory. Import the electronic bank statement through the menu *Accounting → Periodical Processing → Statements → Import Coda Statements*.

Enter the data required in the wizard (receivable and payable account, bank journal and a default account to post to when no corresponding partner is found). Then select the CODA file in your directory and click the `Import` button to start processing the CODA file.

OpenERP will then import a draft bank statement in the selected journal and will match all corresponding customer / supplier payments when possible. You can change the draft statement if necessary from the menu *Accounting → Bank and Cash → Bank Statements*. You can check any issues during file loading from the menu *Accounting → Bank and Cash → Coda Import Logs*.

Get your Money in 4

OpenERP provides many tools for managing customer and supplier accounts. In this part we will explain:

- financial analysis of partners, to understand the reports that enable you to carry out an analysis of all of your partners,

- multi-level reminders, which is an automatic system for preparing reminder letters or emails when invoices remain unpaid,

- detailed analysis of individual partners.

4.1 Financial Analysis of Partners

When members of your accounting department sign in to OpenERP, they can immediately be presented with the *Accounting Dashboard*. By default, it contains the customer invoices to approve, a company analysis according to account type, a Treasury graph and a useful graph for analyzing aged receivables. Click the Accounting button in the top toolbar to open the dashboard. You can also call the dashboard from the menu *Accounting → Reporting → Dashboard → Accounting Dashboard*. In the dashboard, the graph at the right entitled *Aged Receivables* represents your receivables week by week. At a glance, you can see the cumulative amount of what your customers owe you by week.

All of OpenERP's graphs are dynamic. So you can, for example, filter the data by clicking the graph itself and then *Filter* in the Search form. When you click the graph, data will be displayed in list view. Now you enter extra search criteria and then click the *graph* button to display the data as a graph again.

To obtain a more detailed report of the aged balance (or order by past date), use the menu *Accounting → Reporting → Generic Reporting → Partners → Aged Partner Balance*.

When you click that report, OpenERP shows a wizard asking you for the chart of accounts, the start date of the analysis period and the size of the interval to be analysed (in days). The start date will determine which documents will be included in the report (document date until the selected start date) and it will serve as a reference date to calculate the amounts due for the selected interval. You can print an aged partner balance for Receivable Accounts or Payable Accounts of for both at the same time. The analysis direction may be Past (for entries that are due) or Future to keep track of your cash flow in the next days or weeks (according to your selection). OpenERP then calculates a table of credit balance by period. So, if you request an interval of 30 days, OpenERP generates an analysis of creditors for the past month, past two months, and so on. An ageing balance will indicate how much of the accounts receivable is overdue. It also reports how far overdue the accounts are (number of days).

Aged Partner Balance

This report works best of you use payment terms or if you set a due date yourself.

Aged Trial Balance

Chart of Accounts	Fiscal Year	Start Date	Period Length(days)	Partner's	Analysis Direction	Target Moves
Your Company	Fiscal Year 2011	10/17/2011	30	Receivable Accounts	past	All Posted Entries

Partners	Not due	0-30	30-60	60-90	90-120	+120	Total
Account Total	0.00 €	3500.00 €	1089.00 €	0.00 €	0.00 €	0.00 €	4589.00 €
Axelor	0.00 €	0.00 €	1089.00 €	0.00 €	0.00 €	0.00 €	1089.00 €
Ecole de Commerce de Liege	0.00 €	3500.00 €	0.00 €	0.00 €	0.00 €	0.00 €	3500.00 €

Figure 4.1: *Aged Balance in the Past using a 30-days Period*

Aged Trial Balance

Chart of Accounts	Fiscal Year	Start Date	Period Length(days)	Partner's	Analysis Direction	Target Moves
Your Company	Fiscal Year 2011	10/17/2011	30	Receivable Accounts	future	All Posted Entries

Partners	Due	0-30	30-60	60-90	90-120	+120	Total
Account Total	1089.00 €	3500.00 €	0.00 €	0.00 €	0.00 €	0.00 €	4589.00 €
Axelor	1089.00 €	0.00 €	0.00 €	0.00 €	0.00 €	0.00 €	1089.00 €
Ecole de Commerce de Liege	0.00 €	3500.00 €	0.00 €	0.00 €	0.00 €	0.00 €	3500.00 €

Figure 4.2: *Aged Balance in the Future using a 30-days Period*

For an analysis by partner, you can use the partner balance that you get through the menu *Accounting → Reporting → Generic Reporting → Partners → Partner Balance*. The system then supplies you with a PDF report containing one line per partner representing debit, credit and balance. The total is displayed per account receivable.

Partner Balance

Chart of Accounts	Fiscal Year	Journals	Filter By	Partner's	Target Moves
Your Company	Fiscal Year 2011	TSAJ, TSCNJ, TEXJ, TECNJ, TBNK, TCHK, TCSH, TMIS, TOEJ, STJ, SAJ, EXJ, SCNJ, ECNJ, MISC, BNK1, as	No Filter	Receivable Accounts	All Posted Entries

Code	(Account/Partner) Name	Debit	Credit	Balance	In dispute
Total:		4589.00	0.00	4589.00 €	0.00 €
400000	Clients	4589.00	0.00	4589.00 €	0.00 €
	Axelor	1089.00	0.00	1089.00 €	0.00 €
	Ecole de Commerce de Liege	3500.00	0.00	3500.00 €	0.00 €

Figure 4.3: *Partner Balance*

If you want detailed information about all invoices, credit notes and payments related to partner, print the partner ledger from the menu *Accounting → Reporting → Generic Reporting → Partners → Partner Ledger*. You can choose to print one partner per page.

Furthermore, OpenERP also provides statistics about individual account entries, invoices and treasury, for instance. To look up statistic information about your accounting, explore the menu *Accounting → Reporting → Statistic Reports*. There you will find Invoices Analysis, Entries Analysis

Partner Ledger

	Chart of Accounts	Fiscal Year	Journals	Filters By	Partner's	Target Moves
	Your Company	Fiscal Year 2011	TSAJ, TSCNJ, TEXJ, TECNJ, TBNK, TCHK, TCSH, TMIS, TOEJ, STJ, SAJ, EXJ, SCNJ, ECNJ, MISC, BNK1, as	No Filter	Receivable Accounts	All Posted Entries

Date	JRNL	Ref	Account	Entry Label	Debit	Credit	Balance
- Ecole de Commerce de Liege					**3500.00**	**0.00**	**3500.00 €**
10/17/2011	SAJ	SAJ/2011/0002	400000	SAJ2011... - /	1500.00	0.00	1500.00 €
10/17/2011	SAJ	SAJ/2011/0001	400000	SAJ2011... - /	2000.00	0.00	3500.00 €
- Axelor					**1089.00**	**0.00**	**1089.00 €**
08/09/2011	SAJ	SAJ/2011/0003	400000	Ageing - Ageing	1089.00	0.00	1089.00 €

Figure 4.4: *Partner Ledger*

and `Treasury Analysis` to name some. By default these statistics are displayed as a list which you can filter to fit your needs. Standard filter buttons, extended filters and grouping features allow you to make an in-depth analysis of your accounting. But the list is not all OpenERP has to offer. These statistic reports can be displayed as a graph simply by clicking the `Graph` button at the top right side of the screen. Notice that graphs allow for only one Group by function at a time.

Figure 4.5: *Entries Analysis List View*

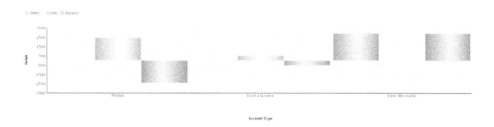

Figure 4.6: *Entries Analysis Graph View*

Exporting Entries

Remember that you can export all types of resources in OpenERP. From the web client, you need to navigate to a search list for the resource, then click the *Export* link at the bottom left of the list. From the GTK client, you would use the menu *Form → Export data*. The Export feature enables you to easily create your own analysis in tools such as Microsoft Excel or Calc (LibreOffice or OpenOffice), simply by exporting accounting entries.

4.2 Multi-step Reminders

To automate the management of follow-ups (reminders) you should install the module `account_followup` (or check the *Followups Management* option in the *Add More Features* wizard).

This module is integrated with the email features of OpenERP. Ask your system administrator to define the smtp server through the menu *Settings → Configuration → Email → Outgoing Mail Servers*.

Once the module is installed, configure your levels of follow-up using the menu *Accounting → Configuration → Miscellaneous → Follow-Ups*.

Follow-ups

You can define only one follow-up cycle per company, because you cannot link the follow-up cycle to a partner.

The levels of follow-up are relative to the due date; when no payment term is specified, the invoice date will be considered as the due date.

For each level, you should define the number of days and create a note which will automatically be added into the reminder letter. The order in which you define the various follow-up levels determines the order in which letters will be sent.

Table 4.1: Example of Configuring Follow-up Levels

Sequence	Level	Days	Description
1	Level 1	15 days net	First payment reminder
2	Level 2	30 days net	Second reminder
3	Level 3	45 days from end of month	Put on notice

You can send your reminders by mail and/or email with the menu *Accounting → Periodical Processing → Billing → Send followups*.

OpenERP allows you to plan your reminders in the future; you could start a cycle today for invoices due at the end of the week, for instance. OpenERP presents you with a list of partners who are due to

Figure 4.7: *Prepare Reminders*

be reminded, which you can modify before starting the procedure. On the `Email Settings` tab of the form, you can supply the information you will send in the email reminder.

You can either print the reminders or send them by email. From the `Email Settings` tab, you can select the `Test Print` checkbox to print the reminders as a preview only, without adding follow-up data to the reminded invoices. This way you can easily preview reminders to be sent.

The system then gives you a PDF report with all of the reminder letters for each partner. Each letter is produced in the language of the partner (if that is specified), so it is possible to have letters in different languages in the same PDF on several pages.

From the `Journal Items` view, you can check the due date of customers before starting the reminder procedure. You will get a list of unreconciled entries only by clicking the `Unreconciled` button. The best thing to do is open the unreconciled line in Form view; select the line and click the `Form` button at the top of the page. You can then easily modify the duedate, the last follow-up and the reminder level for each entry.

To obtain a detailed statistical report of sent follow-ups go to the menu *Accounting* → *Reporting* → *Generic Reporting* → *Partners* → *Follow-ups Sent*. This screen will let you analyse your reminder data in various ways, e.g. by follow-up level, by partner or for a combination of these data. You can also group by `Latest Followup Date` or `Partner`, for instance.

The different reports are standard OpenERP screens, so you can filter them and explore the elements in detail.

Figure 4.8: *Reminder Statistics*

Analyse your Turnover 5

Analyse your invoicing in OpenERP through the **Invoices Analysis** screen from the menu *Accounting → Reporting → Statistic Reports → Invoices Analysis*.

In this statistic report, the columns displayed will vary according to the selections and grouping made, thus making it a very flexible report to analyse your invoices.

This report provides an overview of what has been invoiced to your customer as well as the average payment delays. To see the average due delay, make sure to group by Due Date. You can easily group by partner, product category, ... or select only invoices that have not been confirmed yet.

This is also an easy way to check your sales people's impact on turnover. You can see your turnover per product category, per salesman, per partner and many more options.

Figure 5.1: *Analysing your Invoices*

To quickly see the total turnover per customer in a graph view, group by Partner and click the Graph button to change to graph mode.

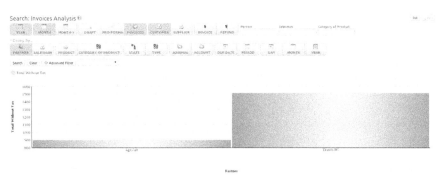

Figure 5.2: *Analysing your Customer's Turnover*

Part IV

Accounting Management

This chapter traces the accounting workflow in OpenERP, from entering an invoice to registering payments. The various operations are described, from the entry of accounting receipts to the treatment of the reconciliation process, including payment orders.

Accounting is at the heart of managing a company: all the company's operations have an impact here. It has an informational role (how much cash is there? what debts need to be repaid?) and, because of the information it provides, a reliable and detailed accounting system can and should have a major decision-making role.

In most companies, accounting is limited to producing statutory reports and satisfying the directors' curiosity about certain strategic decisions, and to printing the balance sheet and the income statement several times a year. Even then, there is often several weeks of delay between reality and the report.

Valueing your Accounting Function

In many small companies, the accounting function is poorly treated.

Not only do you see the data for documents being entered into the system twice, but also the results are often just used to produce legal documents and regular printouts of the balance sheet and income statements some weeks after the closing dates.

By contrast, integrating your accounts with your management system means that you can:

- reduce data entry effort – you only need to do it once,

- run your processes with the benefit of financial vision: for example, in managing projects, negotiating contracts, and forecasting cash flow,

- easily get hold of useful information when you need it, such as a customer's credit position.

So accounting is too often underused. The information it brings makes it a very effective tool for running the company if accounting is integrated into the management system. Financial information really is necessary in all of your company's processes for you to be effective, for example:

- to prepare quotations, the precise financial position of the customer is a key element, as well as history of any delays in payment,

- if a given customer has exceeded his credit limit, accounting can automatically stop further deliveries to the customer,

- if a project budget is 80% consumed, but the project is only 20% complete, you could renegotiate with the customer, or review the objectives of the project,

- if you need to improve your company's cash flow, you could plan your service projects on the basis of invoicing rates and payment terms of the various projects, and not just delivery dates – you could work on short-term customer projects as opposed to R&D projects, for example.

OpenERP's general and analytic accounting handle these needs well because of the close integration between all of the application modules. Furthermore, the transactions, the actions and the financial analyses happen in real time, so that you cannot only monitor the situation, but also manage it effectively. Financial Management in OpenERP covers general accounting, analytic accounting, auxiliary and budgetary accounting. It is double-entry, multi-currency and multi-company.

 Accounting

- General accounting (or financial accounting) is for identifying the assets and liabilities of the business. It is managed using double-entry accounting which ensures that each transaction is credited to one account and debited from another.

- Analytic accounting (also called management or cost accounting) is an independent accounting system, which reflects the general accounts but is structured along axes that represent the company's management needs.

- Auxiliary accounting reflects the accounts of customers and/or suppliers.

- Budgetary accounts predefine the expected allocation of resources, usually at the start of a financial year.

Multi-company

There is a choice of methods for integrating OpenERP in a multi-company environment:

- if the companies hold few documents in common (such as products, or partners - any OpenERP resource), you could install separate databases,

- if the companies share many documents, you can register them in the same database and add OpenERP's multi-company user group to finely manage access rights,

One of the great advantages of integrating accounts with all of the other modules is in avoiding the double entry of data into accounting documents. So in OpenERP, an Order automatically generates an Invoice, and the Invoice automatically generates the accounting entries. These in turn generate tax submissions, customer reminders, and so on. Such strong integration enables you to:

- reduce data entry work,

- greatly reduce the number of data entry errors,

- get information in real time and enable very fast reaction times (for reminders, for example),

- exert timely control over all areas of company management.

All the accounts are held in the default currency (which is specified in the company definition), but each account and/or transaction can also have a secondary currency (which is defined in the account). The value of multi-currency transactions is then tracked in both currencies.

Advanced Invoice Management   6

The principle of entering data for invoices in OpenERP is very simple, both for people with no background in accounting (see chapter :ref:custinv') and accountants. This means that your accounting information can be kept up-to-date all the time as orders are placed and received, and their taxes are calculated.

People who have more accounting knowledge will be able to keep full control over the accounting entries that are being generated. Each value proposed by OpenERP can be modified later if needed.

In OpenERP, the concept of "invoice" refers to the following documents:

- The Customer Invoice,

- The Supplier Invoice,

- A Customer Credit Note (also called Customer Refund),

- A Supplier Credit Note (also called Supplier Refund).

Only the invoice type and the representation mode are different, but still very similar, for each of the four documents. But they are all stored in the same object type in the system.

Each of the four invoice types is related to a corresponding menu item. This allows you to easily distinguish between them, and also to directly refer to the invoice type you need to work on.

 Credit Note

A credit note is a document that enables you to refund an invoice or part of an invoice.

6.1 Creating a Customer Invoice

To access customer invoices in OpenERP, use the menu *Accounting → Customers → Customer Invoices*; for supplier invoices, go to the menu *Accounting → Suppliers → Supplier Invoices*.

In general, when you also use OpenERP's functionality for sales, purchases and logistics, most of the invoices do not need to be entered manually as they are linked to other processes in the system. Draft invoices are generated automatically by OpenERP from other documents such as Sales Orders, Purchase Orders or Shipments.

OpenERP uses the following ways to generate invoices:

- from purchase or sales orders,

- from receipt or dispatch of goods,

- from work carried out (timesheets),

- from closed tasks (projects),

- from fee charges or other rechargeable expenses (service management).

The chart *Accounting Workflow for Invoicing and Payment* (page 32) shows the financial workflow followed by each invoice.

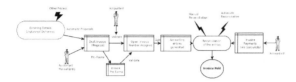

Figure 6.1: *Accounting Workflow for Invoicing and Payment*

The integrated software generates invoice proposals (also called Draft Invoices) which are initially set to the ''Draft'' state, which means they can easily be changed when required. As long as these invoices remain unconfirmed, they have no accounting impact on the system.

Draft sales invoices have to be approved by an accountant or other dedicated users and sent to the customer. The different invoicing methods are detailed in the following sections and chapters.

You can also create invoices manually, both for customers and suppliers. This option is usually used for invoices that are not associated with an order (e.g. purchase invoices for electricity) or credit notes.

Of course, you might need to edit or add extra information to the invoice before sending it to the customer. For example, when setting the tax parameters for partners, you have not realised that the customer is tax-exempt. The invoice generated from an order will contain tax at the normal rates based on system settings for partner, product or account. You can then easily edit the invoice before validating it.

You can create or edit a draft customer invoice manually from the menu *Accounting → Customers → Customer Invoices*.

The information that is needed for invoicing is automatically taken from the `Partner` form (such as payment conditions and the invoice address) or from the `Product` (such as the account to be used) or from a combination of the two (such as applicable Taxes and the Price of the product). From an invoice, you can easily create a new partner, a new product, a new account without having to leave the invoice screen. You can also edit existing data, all from within one form. This makes it very easy to quickly enter invoices.

> **Draft Invoices**
>
> There are several advantages in working with draft invoices:
>
> - You have got an intermediate validation state before the invoice is approved. This is useful when your accountants are not the people creating the initial invoice, but are still required to approve it before the invoice is entered into the accounts.
>
> - It enables you to create invoices in advance, without approving them at the same time. You are also able to list all of the invoices awaiting approval.

You can approve (or *validate*) an invoice to change its status to ''Open''. Clicking the `Pro-forma` button will set the invoice to the ''Pro-forma''status. A pro forma invoice does not have an invoice number yet, nor any accounting entries, and is commonly used as a preliminary invoice or for customs purposes. Such a pro forma invoice is more formal than a draft invoice and can easily be converted to an open invoice when required, simply by clicking the `Validate` button.

An open invoice has a unique invoice number. The invoice is sent to the customer and is marked in the system as awaiting payment.

Start by manually entering a customer invoice. Go to *Accounting → Customers → Customer Invoices* and click the *Create* button.

A new invoice form opens allowing you to enter information.

Figure 6.2: *Entering a New Invoice*

The document is composed of three parts:

- the top of the invoice, with customer information,

- the main body of the invoice, with detailed invoice lines,

- the bottom of the page, with details about taxes and totals and the status of the invoice.

To enter a document in OpenERP, you should try to always fill in the fields in the order they appear on the screen. Doing it this way means that some of the later fields are filled in automatically from the selections made in earlier fields.

The Sales Journal is proposed by default. If you use several sales journals, make sure to select the required journal. Then select the *Customer*, and the following fields will be completed automatically:

- the invoice address: corresponds to the customer contact associated to the *Invoice* address type in the partner form (or otherwise the *Default* address type),

- the account: corresponds to the centralisation account specified in the *Accounting* tab of the *Partner* form,

- a specific or a default payment term: can be defined for the partner in the *Accounting* tab of the *Partner* form. Payment conditions are generated by rules for the payment of the invoice. For example: 50% in 21 days and 50% in 60 days from the end of the month.

You do not have to enter a date and a period, because the system's date and corresponding period will be set automatically on validation. For purchase invoices, set the date specified on the supplier's invoice. The period will be proposed accordingly on validation.

Properties Fields

The Properties fields (fields with default values, such as payment term) on the *Partner* or the *Product* form are multi-company fields. The value the user sees in these fields depends on the company he works for.

If you work in a multi-company environment that is using one database, you have several charts of accounts. Centralisation accounts for a partner depend on the company the user works for.

Seeing Partner Relationships

You can reach more information from certain relation fields in OpenERP.

- In the web client, a relation is commonly a hyperlink that you open by clicking the small button with the hand, next to a field - it takes you to the main form for that entity, with all of the actions and links.

According to the Business Applications you use, one way or another you can rapidly reach the partner's:

- current sales and purchases,

- CRM meetings,

- invoices,

- accounting entries,

- payable and receivable accounts.

You can add more detailed additional information to the invoice and select the currency that you want to invoice in.

For each invoice, you have to enter the different invoice lines. You could use either of the two techniques:

- use a product to complete the different fields automatically;

- use no product, but instead enter all blue (= mandatory) fields manually for one-off sales,

Invoice Line Description

The invoice line description is more of a title than a comment. If you want to add more detailed comments you can use the *Notes* field.

Select the product Basic PC in the product field of an invoice line. You can enter a product code, or part of the name of a product. OpenERP will propose corresponding products. The following fields are then completed automatically:

- *Description*: this comes from the product, in the language of the partner,

- the *Quantity* is set to 1 by default, but can be changed manually,

- Unit of Measure, e.g. PCE, defined by default in the *Product* form,

- *Unit Price*: this is the sales price in the *Product* form or the price from the selected pricelist; the unit price is expressed exclusive of taxes,

- *Account*: the sales account defined in the product properties. If no account is specified in the *Product* form, OpenERP uses the properties of the category the product is associated with.

- *Taxes*: provided by the *Product* form and related to the fiscal position (either from the *Partner* form or added manually to the invoice).

You can add more lines by clicking the `Save & New` button. When you are done entering invoice lines, click the `Save & Close` button.

Managing the Price with Tax Included

By default, OpenERP invoices and processes the price without taxes – they are managed as a separate amount. OpenERP can manage tax-inclusive prices when you check the *Tax Included in Price* field when configuring the tax.

Information about the Product

When you are entering invoice data, it can sometimes be useful to get hold of more information about the product you are invoicing. Note that the options depend on the number of Business Applications installed. Simply click the small button with the hand to select the available reports. OpenERP provides three standard reports about the product:

- forecasts of future stock,

- product cost structure,

- location of the product in your warehouses.

You can enter several invoice lines and modify the default values that are automatically completed by OpenERP. Do not forget to change the default quantity of 1 to the correct quantity.

Once the invoice lines have been entered, you can click *Compute Taxes* on the invoice to get the following information:

- details of tax calculated,

- tax rate,

- total taxes,

- total price.

In the *Taxes* area at the bottom left of the invoice you will find the details of the totals calculated for different tax rates used in the invoice.

Tax Calculations

When the invoice is not in `Edit` mode, you can click one of the lines in the tax summary area in the invoice.

OpenERP then shows you the detail of the tax charges which will be used to compute your tax declaration at the end of the period.

It shows you the total that will be computed in the different parts of the legal declaration. This enables you to manage the declaration in OpenERP automatically.

Close

Tax Description : VAT-OUT-21-L - VAT 21%   Sequence : 11

Tax Account : 451054 T.V.A. a payer   Manual :

Amount : 94.50   Base : 450.00

Tax codes

Base Code : 03 - Opérations avec TVA a 21%   Base Code Amount : 450.00

Tax Code : 54 - TVA sur operations des grilles [01], [02], [03]   Tax Code Amount : 94.50

Figure 6.3: *Detail of Tax Charges on an Invoice*

On the second tab *Other Info*, you can change the due date of the invoice (automatically proposed according to the payment terms). You can also select a salesman, if it has not been set by default for the customer. A proposed salesman can also be changed for the invoice.

Before approving the invoice you can modify the date and the accounting period, which will be set by default to today's date on confirmation of the invoice.

 Invoice Layout

If you want to make your invoice layout more elaborate you can install the module `account_invoice_layout`. This enables you to add various elements between the lines such as subtotals, sections, separators and notes.

Click *Validate* when you want to approve the invoice. It moves from the `Draft` state to the `Open` status. You can easily see the current status of the invoice through the coloured status fields (blue for draft, grey for open) at the bottom of the screen.

When you have validated an invoice, OpenERP attributes a unique number from a defined sequence (see `Number` field). By default, it takes the form `Journal Code/Year/Sequence Number` for example, `saj/2011/005` . You cannot modify an invoice number. Instead, to get a number that corresponds to your needs, you should modify the sequence numbers through the menu *Settings → Configuration → Sequences & Identifiers → Sequences*.

Accounting entries corresponding to this invoice are automatically generated when you approve the invoice. Have a look at the details by clicking the small button with the hand next to the *Journal Entry* field on the *Other Info* tab (when the invoice is in `Edit` mode). When the invoice is not in `Edit` mode, simply click the entry number next to the *Journal Entry* field. Here you can see the account moves generated by that invoice number.

The `Print Invoice` button allows you to print the validated invoice. Automatically, the invoice will be stored as an attachment. When the edi module is configured (read more about it in this book), the invoice will be emailed to the customer on validation.

Occasional Invoices

When you create an invoice for a product that will only be sold once, you do not have to encode a new product. Instead, you will have to provide quite a bit of information manually in the invoice line, especially the blue or mandatory fields:

- sales price,

- applicable taxes,

- account,

- product description.

6.2 Tax Management

Taxes can be defined from the *Accounting → Configuration → Financial Accounting → Taxes → Taxes* menu. OpenERP not only allows you to define general sales and purchase taxes, but also specific taxes, such as ecological taxes, that should be added to a product together with the default tax.

You can combine as many taxes as required for an invoice line. For further details about tax definition, please refer to the chapter *Managing your Tax Structure* (page 131).

Default taxes can be added to a product or to a general account (mostly for purchase invoices). One of the main options to determine the applicable taxes for an invoice line, are the taxes defined in the *Product* form. By default, OpenERP takes account of all the taxes defined in the product form. This means you can easily add several legal taxes to one product, such as the Belgian Recupel (collection of waste electronic and electric material) and Bebat (battery) taxes.

Take the case of the following product:

- Applicable taxes:

    - VAT: 19.6% type VAT
    - DEEE: 5.5, type DEEE

DEEE Tax

The DEEE tax (disposal of electronic and electrical equipment) is an ecological tax that was imposed in France from 2009. It is applied to batteries to finance their recycling and is a fixed sum that is applied to the before-tax amount on the invoice.

If you trade with a company in your own country, and your country has a DEEE-type tax, the applicable taxes for this invoice could be:

- DEEE: 5.5,

- VAT: 19.6%.

If you sell to a customer in another company of the European community (intracommunity) instead, then tax is not charged. In the partner form, in the tab *Accounting*, the *Fiscal Position* field keeps information about whether the customer is a local, an intracommunal or an export customer. When you create an invoice for this customer, OpenERP will calculate the following taxes on the product:

- DEEE: 5.5,

- Intracommunal VAT: 0%.

If you have not entered the parameters in the customer form correctly, OpenERP will suggest incorrect taxes in the invoice. That is not a real issue, because you can always modify the information directly in the *Fiscal Position* field of the invoice before approving it.

If you do not enter a product in the invoice line, but instead use text, you can easily add taxes manually, or they may be added automatically from the general account if it has been linked to default taxes.

6.3 Cancelling an Invoice

By default, OpenERP will not allow you to cancel an invoice once it has been approved. Since accounting entries have been created, you theoretically cannot go back and delete them. However, in some cases, it is more convenient to cancel an invoice when there is an error than to produce a credit note and reconcile the two entries. Your attitude to this will be influenced by current legislation in your accounting jurisdiction.

OpenERP accommodates either approach. The `account_cancel` module can be installed if in your country it is allowed to cancel an existing invoice, correct it and revalidate it. You have to set up some parameters for this module to work. You need to allow cancellation of entries by checking the *Allow Cancelling Entries* box in the `Journal` corresponding to an invoice. You will then be allowed to cancel the invoice if the following two conditions are met:

1. The accounting entries have not been reconciled or paid: if they have, then you will have to cancel the reconciliation first.

2. The accounting period or the fiscal year has not been closed yet: if it is closed, no modification is possible.

When you cancel an invoice, the corresponding accounting entries will automatically be modified accordingly.

You can cancel an invoice by clicking the *Cancel* button in the invoice form. You could then move it from `Cancelled` to the `Draft` state to modify it. Once you have made the required changes, you have to regenerate the invoice by clicking the *Validate* button. Note that the original invoice number will still be used for this invoice.

Numbering Invoices

Some countries require you to have contiguously numbered invoices (that is, with no break in the sequence). If, after cancelling an invoice that you are not regenerating, you find yourself with a break in the numbering, you should modify the sequence, redo the invoice and replace the sequence number with its original value.

You can control the sequences using the menu *Settings → Configuration → Sequences & Identifiers → Sequences*.

Cancelling an invoice without regenerating it, will cause a break in the number sequence of your invoices. You are strongly advised to recreate this invoice and reapprove it to fill the hole in the numbering.

6.4 Controlling a Supplier Invoice

The form that manages supplier invoices is very similar to the one for customer invoices. However, it has been adapted to simplify rapid data entry and monitoring of the amounts recorded.

Entering Data

Many companies do not enter data through supplier invoices, but simply enter accounting data corresponding to the purchase journal.

This particularly applies to users that have focused on the accounting system rather than all the capabilities provided by an ERP system. The two approaches reach the same accounting result: some prefer one and others prefer the other depending on their skills and needs.

However, when you use the Purchase Management functions in OpenERP you should work directly on invoices because they are created from Purchase Orders or Goods Receipt documents.

To enter a new supplier invoice, use the menu *Accounting → Suppliers → Supplier Invoices*.

Everything is similar to the customer invoice, starting with the *Journal* unless the default journal is acceptable, and then the *Supplier*, which will automatically complete the following fields:

- *Invoice Address*,

- Partner *Account*.

Unlike the customer invoice, you do not have to enter payment conditions (although you can, of course) – simply a *Due Date* will do. If you do not give a due date, OpenERP assumes that this invoice will be paid in cash. If you want to enter more complete payment conditions than just the due date, you can use the *Payment Term* field which you can find on the second tab *Other Info*.

You can also store the supplier's invoice number in the *Free Reference* field. You also have to enter the invoice's *Verification Total* amount, taxes included. OpenERP uses this amount to check whether all invoice lines have been entered correctly before it will let you validate the invoice.

Indicate the *Currency* if the invoice is not going to use the default currency, then you can enter the *Invoice lines*.

Just like the customer invoice, you have the choice of entering all the information manually or use a product to complete many of the fields automatically. When you enter a product, all of the following values are completed automatically:

- the product *Account* is completed from the properties of the product form or the *Category* of the product if nothing is defined on the product itself,

- the *Taxes* come from the product form and/or the general account, based on the same principles as the customer invoice,

- the *Quantity* is set at 1 by default but can be changed manually,

- set the *Unit Price* according to the total price on the invoice after deducting all the different applicable taxes (so the amount exclusive of taxes),

Click *Compute Taxes* to ensure that the totals correspond to those indicated on the paper invoice from the supplier. When you approve the invoice, OpenERP verifies that the total amount indicated in the header corresponds to the sum of the amounts exclusive of tax in the invoice lines plus the different applicable taxes.

 Invoice Date

OpenERP automatically completes the *Date Invoiced* and the accounting period on validation, so make sure to enter the invoice date indicated on your supplier invoice before validating.

Dates and Accounting Periods

Accounting periods are treated as legal periods. For example, a tax declaration for an invoice depends on the accounting period and not on the date of invoicing.

Depending on whether you have monthly or quarterly declarations, the fiscal year generally contains either twelve or four accounting periods. We do not take into account any opening / closing periods here.

The dates are shown in the document you created in the accounting system. They are used to calculate due dates.

You may find that the amounts do not correspond with what your supplier has given you on paper for reasons that may include:

- the supplier made a calculation error,

- the amounts have been rounded differently.

Rounding Tax

It often happens that a supplier adds 1 to the total because the tax calculation has been rounded upwards. Some tax amounts are not valid because of this rounding.

For example, it is impossible to arrive at the amount of 145.50 if you are working with a precision of 2 decimal places and a rate of 19.6%:

- $121.65 \times 1.196 = 145.49$

- $121.66 \times 1.196 = 145.51$

In this case, you can modify a value in the lines the total is based on, or the total amount of taxes at the bottom left of the form (in the tax box): both are editable so that you can modify them to adjust the total.

When the totals tally, you can validate the invoice. OpenERP then generates the corresponding accounting entries. You can manage those entries using the *Account* fields on the invoice and on each of the invoice lines.

In a logistic configuration, invoice control for purchase invoices can be done either according to the purchase order, or the picking. When invoicing is from the purchase order, a draft invoice will be created on confirmation of the purchase order. This allows the accountant to easily check the purchase order against the invoice received from the supplier without actually looking at the purchase order. When invoicing is done from the picking, an invoice will be created as soon as the picking is confirmed. This allows the accountant to easily check the picking list against the invoice received from the supplier without actually looking at the picking list.

6.5 Credit Notes / Refunds

Entering a customer credit note is almost identical to entering a customer invoice. You just start from the menu *Accounting → Customers → Customer Refunds*.

Similarly, entering a supplier credit note is the same as that of the supplier invoice, and so you use the menu *Accounting → Suppliers → Supplier Refunds*.

Of course with OpenERP you can quickly generate a credit note from an existing invoice. To do this, select the customer or supplier invoice that has to be refunded, with `Open` or `Paid` status. Click the *Refund* button. OpenERP allows you to select several methods for creating credit notes directly from the related invoice (both for customers and suppliers).

Below you find the different options displayed when you click the *Refund* button on an invoice.

Create a Draft Refund Creates a draft credit note of the complete invoice. You can change this credit note, i.e. to make a partial credit note.

Modify Creates a credit note for the existing invoice, validates the credit note and reconciles it with the invoice. The existing invoice is duplicated so that you can modify it.

Cancel Creates a credit note for the complete invoice, validates the credit note and reconciles it with the invoice concerned. The existing invoice is "cancelled" in a legal way.

Figure 6.4: *Refund from an Invoice*

6.6 Advanced Setup: Payment Terms and Fiscal Positions

Payment Terms

You can define whatever payment terms you need in OpenERP. Payment terms determine the due dates for paying an invoice.

To define new payment terms, go to the menu *Accounting → Configuration → Miscellaneous → Payment Terms* and click *Create*.

The figure below represents the following payment term: 5000 within 5 days, 50% payment at the last day of current month, remaining balance the 15th of next month.

Figure 6.5: *Configuring Payment Terms*

To configure new conditions, start by giving the condition a name in the *Payment Term* field. Text you put in the field *Description on invoices*, will be printed on the invoice, so enter a clear description of the payment terms there.

Then create individual lines to allow the system to automatically calculate the due dates in the section *Computation*. You should give each line a name (*Line Name*). The name is for information only and does not affect the actual computation of payment terms. The *Sequence* field lets you define the order in which the rules are evaluated.

Drag & Drop

You can leave the sequence number to the default value and easily drag and drop payment term lines to change the computation order. Sequence numbers will then be updated automatically.

The *Valuation* field enables you to calculate the amount to pay for each line according to three options:

- `Percent`: the line corresponds to a percentage of the total amount, the factor being specified in *Amount To Pay*. The number indicated in *Amount To Pay* has to take a value between 0 and 1 (1 equals 100%, 0,50 means 50%).

- `Fixed Amount`: this is a fixed value determined by the *Amount To Pay* box.

- `Balance`: refers to the balance remaining after accounting for the other lines.

Make sure to set the last line of the computation to `Balance` to avoid rounding errors. The highest sequence number will be the last to be evaluated.

The last two fields, *Number of Days* and *Day of the Month*, enable the calculation of the delay in payment for each line. The delay *Day of the Month* can be set to −1 , 0 , 1 or any other positive or negative number.

Example starting from 20th December 2011, with the following payment term:

- *5000 within 5 days*: set *Valuation* to `Fixed Amount`, *Amount To Pay* to 5000, *Number of Days* 5 and *Day of the Month* 0. That creates a journal entry with a due date of 25th December 2011.

- *50% last day of current month*: set *Valuation* to `Percent`, *Amount To Pay* to `0.50`, *Number of Days* `0` and *Day of the Month* `-1`. That creates a journal entry with a due date of 31st December 2011.

- *Remaining 15th of next month*: set *Valuation* to `Balance`, *Number of Days* `0` and *Day of the Month* `15`. That creates a journal entry with a due date of 15th January 2012.

What do the digits in the *Day of Month* field represent?

- -1 = last day of the current month

- 0 = net days

- 1 = first day of the next month

- -2 = last but one day of the current month

- 2 = second day of the next month

- 30 = 30th of the next month

- -30 = 30th of the current month

You can add default payment terms to a customer or supplier through the *Accounting* tab in the *Partner* form. On an invoice level, you can change the default payment terms.

Fiscal Positions

The basic configuration of products, for instance, will only take into account local taxes. But of course, you would like OpenERP to determine the corresponding taxes for you when you are invoicing to a customer within the European Community, to give an example.

Now that is what fiscal positions can be used for. Through fiscal positions, you can instruct OpenERP to use the correct taxes. Fiscal positions allow you to make a mapping from e.g. national taxes to intracommunal or external taxes. Moreover, these mappings also allow you to change income / expense accounts automatically when posting entries. An example of this: suppose you have an income account for local sales, one for intracommunal sales and one for export. By defining fiscal positions, you can have the system change the income account automatically.

You can link fiscal positions to your customers and suppliers to ensure automatic and easy VAT and/or account conversion.

To create a new fiscal position, go to *Accounting* → *Configuration* → *Financial Accounting* → *Taxes* → *Fiscal Positions* and click *Create*.

Create for instance a fiscal position for Intracommunal Taxes.

Type Intracommunal Taxes in the *Fiscal Position* field. In the *Tax Source* field, select the local tax that has to be converted for use with intracommunal partners. Then link the intracommunal tax to be used in the *Replacement Tax* field. Do this for each local tax that has to be converted for intracommunal use. If you also want accounts to be changed, you can add *Account Source* (the local account) and *Account Destination* (intracommunal account).

Figure 6.6: *Fiscal Position*

Advanced Cash Management 7

Various methods can be used to create accounting entries. You have already seen how an invoice creates its own entries, for example.

In this section we will explain how you can manage other accounting entries, such as:

- bank statements,

- cash,

- manual journal entries.

In this chapter we will show you how to enter financial transactions. In OpenERP, you can handle bank statements and you can keep a cash register. Use different journals for these two kinds of transaction, i.e. a journal of the *Bank and Cheques* type for bank statements, and a journal of the *Cash* type if you keep a cash register. According to the journal type selected, you will have a different screen. For more information about creating journals, refer to the *Configuring Accounts from A to Z* (page 127) chapter.

7.1 Managing Bank Statements

OpenERP provides a visual tool for managing bank statements that simplifies data entry into accounts. As soon as a statement is validated, the corresponding accounting entries are automatically generated by OpenERP. Also non-accounting people can enter financial transactions without having to worry about things such as credit, debit and counterparts. In a bank statement, you can enter positive amounts if you gain money with a transaction and negative amounts if you pay money from your account.

To enter a bank statement, go to the menu *Accounting* → *Bank and Cash* → *Bank Statements*. Click *Create* to open a data entry form for bank statements, as shown in figure *Registering a Bank Statement* (page 47).

Figure 7.1: *Registering a Bank Statement*

The statement reference *Name* and the *Date* are automatically suggested by OpenERP. The *Name* will be filled with the statement number at confirmation of the bank statement. You can configure your own reference by managing sequences in the *Settings* → *Configuration* → *Sequences & Identifiers* menu.

Then select the correct *Journal*. Ideally, when you are configuring your company, you would create at least one journal for each bank account and one journal for petty cash in your company. So select the journal corresponding to the bank account whose statement you are handling.

The currency you are using for the statement line is that of the selected journal. If you are entering statement lines for an account in US Dollars (USD), the amounts have to be entered in USD . The currency is automatically converted into the company's main currency when you confirm the entry, using the rates in effect at the date of entry. (This means that you would need valid currency conversion rates to be created first. Go to *Accounting → Configuration → Miscellaneous → Currencies* menu.)

OpenERP automatically completes the initial balance based on the closing balance of the preceding statement. You can modify this value and force another value. This lets you enter statements in the order of your choice. Also if you have lost a page of your statement, you can enter the following ones immediately and you are not forced to wait for a duplicate from the bank.

Enter the closing balance which corresponds to the new value in the account displayed on your bank statement. This amount will be used to control the operations before approving the statement.

Then you have to enter all the lines in the statement. Each line corresponds to a banking transaction indicated on your paper statement.

Enter the transaction line. You have two ways of entering financial transactions: manually or through the *Import Invoices* button.

Manual Entry

Remember that blue fields are mandatiry fields and require a value to be filled. When you type the *Partner* name, OpenERP automatically proposes the corresponding centralisation account. Check whether the proposed payment type is correct. *Customer* will be used to register customer payments, while *Supplier* will be used for supplier payments. *General* can be used to enter banking costs, for instance.

You should then enter the amount that appears on your statement line: add a negative sign for a withdrawal (for instance, a supplier payment) and a positive sign for a cash payment or deposit.

In the *Payment* select *Create and Edit* to reconcile your payment directly with the corresponding accounting entry or entries to be paid.

Import Invoices

Click the *Import Invoices* button, then click *Add* to get a list of invoices for which your payment will have to be reconciled. Tick the checkbox in front of each invoice you need and click *Select*. Click *OK* to confirm your selection; the statement line will automatically be added with the corresponding reconciliation.

Figure 7.2: *Reconciliation from the Bank Statement*

Reconciliation

Other methods of reconciliation are possible: from manual accounting entries, when saving the payment directly on an invoice, through *Customer Payment* or *Supplier Payment* or using the automatic reconciliation tool.

You can carry out either a full or a partial reconciliation.

If there is a difference between the payment and the invoices to reconcile, you can enter the difference in the second part of the form *Write-off*. You have to set an account for the adjustment. The main reasons explaining the difference are usually:

- profit or loss,

- exchange differences,

- discounts given for fast payment.

When the reconciliation is complete - that is, the payment is equal to the sum of the due payments and the adjustments - you can close the reconciliation form.

The reconciliation operation is optional – you could very well do it later or not do it at all. However, reconciliation has got two significant effects:

- marking that the invoices have been paid,

- preventing the payment and invoice amounts from appearing on customer reminder letters. Unless you have reconciled them, a customer will see the invoice and payment amounts on his reminder letter (which will not alter the balance due since they will just cancel each other out).

Finally, once you have entered the complete bank statement, you can validate it. OpenERP then automatically generates the corresponding accounting entries if the calculated balance equals the final balance, indicated in the *Ending Balance* field. The reconciled invoices are marked as paid at that point.

You can also enter general accounting entries, for example, banking costs. In such cases, you can enter the amounts directly in the corresponding general accounts with the *General* type selected.

A user with advanced accounting skills can enter accounting entries directly into the bank journal from *Accounting → Journal Entries -> Journal Items*. The result is the same, but the operation is more complex because you have to know the accounts to use and master the ideas of credit and debit.

7.2 Cash Register Management

To manage your cash register, you can use the menu *Accounting → Bank and Cash → Cash Registers*. At the start of the day you set the opening amount of cash in the entry (*Opening Balance*). Then open the cashbox to start making entries from the *Cash Transactions* tab. Enter, for instance, -20 because you bought stamps from the cashbox.

Figure 7.3: *Cash Register*

All the transactions throughout the day can then be entered in this statement. When you close the cashbox, generally at the end of the day, enter the amounts on the *CashBox* tab, in the *Closing Balance* section. Then confirm the statement to close the day's cash statement and automatically generate the corresponding accounting entries. Note that the *Computed Balance* and the *Closing Balance* need to be equal before you can close the cashbox.

Confirming the Statement

Accounting entries are only generated when the cash statement is confirmed. So if the total statement has not been approved (that is to say during the day, in the case of petty cash), partner payments will not have been deducted from their corresponding account.

7.3 Miscellaneous Operations

Invoices and statements produce accounting entries in different journals. But you could also create entries directly in a journal (line by line) without using the dedicated journal views. This functionality is often used for miscellaneous entries.

To make manual entries, go to the following menu *Accounting → Journal Entries → Journal Items*. In the *Journal* field from the filter, start typing the journal in which you want to post (OpenERP will autocomplete), as well as the period, then click *Search*. When you select a journal and a period in this filter, you do not have to fill in the journal on each line when posting new entries. Click *Create* to register a miscellaneous entry. Make sure to complete all blue (mandatory) fields. According to the journal settings, counterpart accounts will be proposed automatically.

You can also post miscellaneous entries from the menu *Accounting → Journal Entries → Journal Entries*. Click *Create* and select the journal in which you want to post your miscellaneous entry. In the `Journal Items` block, click *Create* to start entering lines. Enter the required fields, such as *Name* and *Account*, *Debit* or *Credit*. Press the Enter key to confirm your line; the counterpart entry will automatically be proposed. Change it as required or add extra lines to complete your entry.

Figure 7.4: *Miscellaneous Entry through Journal Items*

Click the *Post* button to validate your entry.

Recording Journal Items 8

All the accounting transactions in OpenERP are based on records, whether they are created by an invoice or directly.

Financial statements such as the general ledger, account balance, aged balance (or chronological balance) and the various journals are all based on accounting entries. It does not matter if you generated the entry from an invoice form or directly in the invoice journal. It is the same for the tax declaration and other statutory financial statements.

8.1 Recording Sales Entries through Journal Items

Journal entries can be entered in several ways, either manually or automatically. As discussed in previous chapters, journal entries are generated automatically on confirmation of purchase and sales invoices, for instance. Manual entries can be added through Journal Entries (several entries in one journal) or through Journal Items (line by line, for accountants).

To easily record journal items, configure your sales journal with a default debit and credit income account, which will be proposed automatically. You also need to add a default sales tax to these accounts, which can be done from the menu *Accounting → Configuration → Financial Management → Accounts → Accounts*. Open the income account you added as default debit and credit account. Click the `Add` button in the `Default Taxes` block and select the applicable local tax(es).

Let us give the example of manually entering a sales invoice through *Accounting → Journal Entries → Journal Items*. Note however that these entries are usually generated automatically by OpenERP.

Select the journal in which you want to post entries in the `Journal` box, enter the period and click `Search`. Now click the *Create* button.

Figure 8.1: *Receivable Entry (first line)*

Start by entering the receivable entry (Account Receivable or Customer account). Fill at least the following fields in the following order:

- *Partner*: partner concerned,

- *Name*: description of the invoice line (e.g. `PC2`),

- *Debit* or *Credit*: here you type the debit or credit amount (for sales typically the credit amount). Type the amount inclusive of taxes.

Press the *Enter* key on your keyboard to validate the first line. The next draft move number is assigned to your accounting entry. Your line is then colored red and takes the `Unbalanced` state. When a line is in the draft state, it is not yet reflected in the accounts. OpenERP will not validate that line until the balancing entry is made (so the credit amounts should balance the debit amounts for that set of entries).

OpenERP now automatically proposes the balancing accounting line with the default account from the sales journal and default tax linked to this account.

Figure 8.2: *Automatically proposed Sales Entry (second line)*

Figure 8.3: *Automatically proposed Sales Entry (third line for VAT)*

At this stage you can modify and validate this second line of the account. When you press the *Enter* key on your keyboard to validate the second line, the corresponding tax line will automatically be proposed. Your entry now has status `Valid`. This status indicates that your entry is balanced, but it can still be reviewed.

To actually post this entry, select the lines concerned by checking the corresponding checkboxes and click `Post Journal Entries` at the right side of the screen.

Posting Entries

You can also post your entries from the menu *Accounting → Journal Entries → Journal Entries*. Simply select the green button at the end of a journal entry line. This has the same effect as the `Post Journal Entries` wizard.

Completing a Balancing Entry

If you want to add some other balancing lines you can enter the number of the entry on the new line that you are entering. In such a case the whole line stays Draft until the whole set balances to zero.

8.2 Miscellaneous Operations: Creating an Opening Entry

When you use OpenERP Accounting & Financial Management for the first time, you will have to enter your Opening Balance for your balance sheet accounts. You can do this through a miscellaneous entry. The best thing is to create a specific Opening Journal (see also the *Configuring Accounts from A to Z* (page 127) chapter for more details) and an Opening Period.

Then, each balance sheet account that has a balance in your previous accounting system has to be reopened with the exact same balance. To do this, go to *Accounting → Journal Entries → Journal Entries*, click *Create* and select the Opening Journal and Period. For each account, create a new line and enter the balance (either debit or credit). The counterpart account for such an entry will typically be your Profit & Loss Account (defined in your journal settings).

Once you started to keep your books in OpenERP, opening entries can be generated automatically at the annual closing (see also the *Configuring Accounts from A to Z* (page 127) chapter).

8.3 Journal Entries

To get an overview of existing journal entries or to create new journal entries, go to *Accounting → Journal Entries → Journal Entries*. Journal entries can be generated in two ways: automatically from invoices or manually by entering account lines in a journal.

You can indeed create the accounting records directly, without using the invoice and account statements. Some accountants prefer this approach because they might find it easier to think in terms of accounting records rather than in terms of invoices and payments.

You should really try to use the forms designed for invoices and bank statements rather than manual data entry records, however. These are simpler and are managed within an error-controlling system.

Through this view, you can see each and every entry that has been made in your accounting system, grouped by move number (each journal entry gets an automatic number). If you want to have a look at each individual move line, you should go to *Accounting → Journal Entries → Journal Items*.

From the *State* column, you can check whether the journal entry has already been validated (*Posted*) or not (*Unposted*).

If you want to have a certain journal entry reviewed by someone else (e.g. your accountant if you prepare most of the entries yourself), you can check the *To Review* box. In List view, the *To Review* button allows you to easily look up entries that need a second opinion.

This screen can also be used to group entries, for instance by partner, journal, or period. The order in which you click the *Group by* buttons determines the way your data will be displayed. With the Advanced Filters, you can look up entries according to amount (is equal to, smaller than, greater than, ...). You can also indicate whether Any, All or None of the conditions should match. These extended filters allow you to get a great view on all your accounting entries!

8.4 Manual Reconciliation Process

Reconciliation

Reconciliation links entries in an account that cancel each other out – they are reconciled to each other (sum of credits = sum of debits).

This is generally applied to payments or credit notes against corresponding invoices.

Without the reconciliation process, OpenERP would be incapable of marking invoices that have been paid. Suppose that you have got the following situation for the `Agrolait` customer:

- Invoice 145: 50,

- Invoice 167: 120,

- Invoice 184: 70.

If you receive a payment of 120, OpenERP will delay reconciliation because there is a choice of invoices to pay. It could either reconcile the payment against invoices 145 and 184 or against invoice 167.

Treatment in Lots

Usually, different transactions are grouped together and handled at the same time rather than invoice by invoice. This is called batch work or lot handling.

You can select several documents in the list of invoices: select the checkboxes of the required lines using the web client and click the appropriate shortcut button at the right; or shift-click the lines using the mouse in the GTK client and use the action or print button at the top – these give you a number of possible actions on the selected objects.

This reconciliation transaction can be carried out at various places in the process, depending on your preferences:

- at data entry for the accounting statement,

- manually from the account records,

- automatically using OpenERP's intelligent reconciliation.

The reconciliation operation consists of matching entries in different accounts to indicate that they are related. Generally reconciliation is used for:

- matching invoice entries to payments, so that invoices are marked as paid and customers do not get payment reminder letters for those entries (reconciliation in a customer account),

- matching deposits and cheque withdrawals with their respective payments,

- matching invoices and credit notes to cancel them out.

A reconciliation has to be carried out on a list of accounting entries by an accountant, so that the sum of credits equals the sum of the debits for the matched entries.

Reconciliation in OpenERP can only be carried out in accounts that have been configured as reconcilable (the *Reconcile* field in the *Account* definition).

For manual reconciliation, open the entries for reconciling an account through the menu *Accounting → Periodical Processing → Reconciliation → Manual Reconciliation*.

You can also call up manual reconciliation from the *Journal Items* screen.

Before starting to reconcile entries, print a partner ledger to have a good view on related entries.

Select the account and/or partner for which entries need to be reconciled.

Sorting Entries to be Reconciled

If you only select an account (e.g. account receivable) to be reconciled, you can easily click the *Partner* column to sort the entries by partner. Note that in OpenERP you can click any column heading to sort your data differently. Click once to sort in ascending order and twice to sort in descending order.

OpenERP indicates the sum of debits and credits for the selected entries. When these are equal you can click the *Reconcile Entries* action (at the right side of the screen; when hidden, click the small arrows) to reconcile the entries.

Example Real Case of Using Reconciliation

Suppose that you are entering customer order details. You wonder what is outstanding on the customer account (that is the list of unpaid invoices and unreconciled payments). To review it from the order form, navigate to the *Partner* field, click the button with the hand and select the option *Receivables and Payables*. OpenERP opens a history of unreconciled accounting entries on screen.

Unreconciled Accounting Entries

After running the *Reconcile Entries* wizard, these lines can no longer be selected and will not appear when the entries are listed again. If there is a difference between the two entries, OpenERP suggests you to make an adjustment. This "write-off" is a compensating entry that enables a complete reconciliation. You should therefore specify the journal and the account to be used for the write-off.

For example, if you want to reconcile the following entries:

Table 8.1: Entries for reconciliation

Date	Ref.	Description	Account	Debit	Credit
12 May 11	INV23	Car hire	4010	544.50	
25 May 11	INV44	Car insurance	4010	100.00	
31 May 11	PAY01	Invoices n° 23, 44	4010		644.00

On reconciliation, OpenERP shows a difference of 0.50. At this stage you have two possibilities:

- do not reconcile, and the customer receives a request for 0.50,

- reconcile and accept an adjustment of 0.50 that you will take from the P&L account.

OpenERP generates the following entry automatically:

Table 8.2: Write-off account

Date	Ref.	Description	Account	Debit	Credit
Date	Ref.	Description	Account	Debit	Credit
03 Jun 11	AJ001	Adjustment: profits and losses	4010		0.50
03 Jun 11	AJ001	Adjustment: profits and losses	XXX	0.50	

The two invoices and the payment will be reconciled in the first adjustment line. The two invoices will then automatically be marked as paid.

8.5 Productivity Tips

Creating new Data

To quickly create new information, such as a partner, an account or a product, you can use the small button with the hand. When you click this button, select the *Create* option. Inside a field, instead of simply selecting existing information, you can also select the *Create and Edit* option to create new accounts or partners, for instance.

Related Information

To quickly find related information, for instance for a partner, an account or a product, you can use the small button with the hand. When you click this button, some options related to the object will be displayed, of course taking into account the Business Applications installed.

Duplicating a Document

The duplication function can be applied to all the system documents: you can duplicate anything – a product, an order, an invoice, or a delivery.

Duplicating Invoices

Instead of entering a new invoice each time, you can base an invoice on a similar preceding one and duplicate it. To do this, first search for a suitable existing invoice. Open the selected invoice, then click *Duplicate*. In the GTK client, select *Form → Duplicate* from the top menu.

The duplication creates a new invoice in the `Draft` state. That enables you to modify the invoice before approving it. Duplicating documents in OpenERP is an intelligent function, which enables the duplicated invoice to be given its own sequence number, today's date, and the draft state, even if the preceding invoice has been paid.

Getting Information by Navigating to it

As you are creating an invoice you will often find you need extra information about the partner to help you complete the invoice. As described earlier, you can navigate to other information linked to this partner by clicking the small button with the hand, such as:

- Monthly Turnover
- Benefit Details,
- Most Recent Invoices,
- Receivables & Payables,
- Contracts / Analytic Accounts,
- Latest Orders - Sales Order, Purchase Order.

Please note that the displayed options depend on the number of Business Applications you have installed. Do the same to get information about the products you are invoicing. For example: is there enough stock? When will you be getting more stocks in? What are the costs and normal list prices for this product?

By making this information easily accessible while you are invoicing, OpenERP greatly simplifies your work in creating the invoice.

Find what You Need from a Journal Entry

When you are encoding journal entries, you will see the button with the small hand which allows you to drill down to related information for the field concerned. Below you will see an example of information that can be looked up for a journal, such as Unpaid Invoices and Bank Statements. The drill-down button can be found on many fields, such as account, product, partner, journal, analytic accounts, and more. This button also provides a quick way to check any unreconciled entries for an account.

Clicking the Drill-Down Button for Extra Information

Automate your Payments 9

OpenERP gives you forms to prepare, validate and execute payment orders. This enables you to manage issues such as:

1. Payment provided on several due dates.

2. Automatic payment dates.

3. Separating payment preparation and payment approval in your company.

4. Preparing an order during the week containing several payments, then validating a payment order at the end of the week.

5. Splitting payments depending on the balances available in your various bank accounts.

6. Printing the Payment Order and send it to the bank.

9.1 Supplier Payments

To use the tool for managing payment orders you should first install the module `account_payment` or check the `Supplier Payment Management` option from the *Add More Features* Wizard. Supplier Payments are part of the core OpenERP system.

The system lets you enter a series of payments to be carried out from your various bank accounts. Once the different payments have been registered, you can validate the payment orders. During validation you can modify and approve the payment orders.

For example, if you have to pay a supplier's invoice for a large amount you can split the payments amongst several bank accounts according to their available balance. To do this, you can prepare several draft orders and validate them once you are satisfied that the split is correct.

This process can also be regularly scheduled. In some companies, a payment order is kept in `Draft` state and payments are added to the draft list each day. At the end of the week, the accountant reviews and confirms all the waiting payment orders.

Once the payment order is confirmed, there is still a validation step for an accountant to carry out. You could imagine that these orders would be prepared by an accounts clerk, and then approved by a manager to go ahead with payment.

Payment Workflow

An OpenERP workflow is associated with each payment order. Select a payment order, and if you are in the GTK client click *Plugins → Print workflow* from the top menu.

You can integrate more complex workflow rules to manage payment orders by adapting the workflow. For example, in some companies payments must be approved by a manager under certain cash flow or value limit conditions.

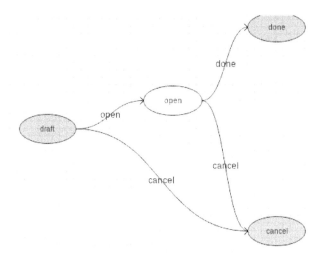

Figure 9.1: *Payments Workflow*

In small businesses it is usually the same person who enters the payment orders and who validates them. In this case you should just click the two buttons, one after the other, to confirm the payment.

First configure the *Payment Modes* you want to use. Consider these as the bank accounts from which you want to pay your suppliers. This can be a bank account or a credit card account to name some. Go to the menu *Accounting → Configuration → Miscellaneous → Payment Mode*. Enter the name of the Payment mode, choose a bank journal and the related bank account (IBAN or normal bank account).

Some examples are:

- Cheques

- Bank transfer,

- Visa card on a bank account,

- Petty cash.

To enter a payment order, go to the menu *Accounting → Payment → Payment Orders* and click Create.

OpenERP proposes a reference number for your payment order; this number can also be changed from the *Administration → Configuration → Sequences & Identifiers → Sequences* menu. Use the sequence of the *Payment Order* type if you want to adapt the reference number that will be proposed automatically for each new payment order.

You then have to select a payment mode from the various methods available for your company (cfr. configuring Payment Modes).

The *Preferred date* for the payment allows you to determine when the payments have to be executed:

Figure 9.2: *Entering a Payment Order*

- Due date: each operation will be effected at the due date specified on the invoice (the default option),

- Directly: the operations will be effected when the orders are validated, i.e. the payment date will be the order validation date,

- Fixed date: you have to specify an effective payment date in the *Scheduled date if fixed* field that follows.

The date is particularly important for the preparation of electronic transfers, because banking interfaces enable you to select a future execution date for each operation. The default option of OpenERP is to pay all invoices automatically at their due date.

Electronic Files

By default, OpenERP does not provide an electronic payment order.

Now select the invoices to pay. Invoices and advance payments (even when not linked to an actual document) can be entered manually in the payment lines block, but you can also add them automatically. Simply click the *Select Invoices to Pay* button and OpenERP will propose documents according to the specified due date. For each due date you can see:

- the invoice *Payment Date*,

- the reference *Invoice Ref.*,

- the deadline for the invoice,

- the amount to be paid in the partner's default currency.

You can then accept the payment proposed by OpenERP, or select the entries that you will pay or not pay on that order. OpenERP gives you all the necessary information to make a payment decision for each line item:

- account,

- supplier's bank account,

- amount that will be paid,

- amount to pay,

- the supplier,

- total amount owed to the supplier,

- due date,

- date of creation.

You can modify the first three fields on each line: the account, the supplier's bank account and the amount that will be paid. This arrangement is very practical because it gives you complete visibility of all the company's trade payables. You can pay only a part of an invoice, for example, and in preparing your next payment order OpenERP automatically suggests payment of the remainder owed.

When the payment has been prepared correctly, click *Confirm Payments*. The payment then changes to the `Confirmed` state and a new button appears that can be used to start the payment process.

You can print the payment order to send it to the bank by clicking the *Payment Order* at the right side of the screen.

9.2 Automatic Reconciliation

For automatic reconciliation, you will be asking OpenERP to search for entries to reconcile in a series of accounts. OpenERP tries to find entries for each partner where the amounts correspond.

Depending on the level of complexity that you choose (= power) when you start running the tool, the software could reconcile from two to nine entries at the same time. For example, if you select level 5, OpenERP will reconcile, for instance, three invoices and two payments if the total amounts correspond. Note that you can also choose a maximum write-off amount, if you allow payment differences to be posted (*Allow write off*).

Figure 9.3: *Automatic Reconciliation*

To start the reconciliation tool, click *Accounting* → *Periodical Processing* → *Reconciliation* → *Automatic Reconciliation*.

A form opens, asking you for the following information:

- *Accounts to Reconcile* : you can select one, several or all reconcilable accounts,
- the dates of the entries to take into consideration (*Starting Date* / *Ending Date*),
- the Reconciliation *Power* (from 2 to 9),
- checkbox *Allow write off* to determine whether you will allow for payment differences.
- information needed for the adjustment (details for the *Write-Off Move*).

Reconciling

You can reconcile any account, but the most common accounts are:

- all the Accounts Receivable – your customer accounts of type Debtor,
- all the Accounts Payable – your supplier accounts of type Creditor.

The write-off option enables you to reconcile entries even if their amounts are not exactly equivalent. For example, OpenERP permits foreign customers whose accounts are in different currencies to have a difference of up to, say, 0.50 units of currency and put the difference in a write-off account.

When you run the wizard, OpenERP will show the reconciliation results in a separate window.

Limit Write-off Adjustments

You should not make the adjustment limits too large. Companies that introduced substantial automatic write-off adjustments have found that all employee expense reimbursements below the limit were written off automatically!

Part V

Analytic Accounts

Sitting at the heart of your company's processes, analytic accounts (or cost accounts) are indispensable tools for managing your operations well. Unlike your financial accounts, they are for more than accountants - they are for general managers and project managers too.

You need a common way of referring to each user, service, or document to integrate all your company's processes effectively. Such a common basis is provided by analytic accounts (or management accounts, or cost accounts, as they are also called) in OpenERP.

Analytic accounts are often presented as a foundation for strategic enterprise decisions. But because of all the information they pull together, OpenERP's analytic accounts can be a useful management tool, at the center of most system processes.

There are several reasons for this:

- they reflect your entire management activity,

- unlike the general accounts, the structure of the analytic accounts is not regulated by legal obligations, so each company can adapt it to its needs.

Independence from General Accounts

In some software packages, analytic accounts are managed as an extension of general accounts – for example, by using the two last digits of the account code to represent analytic accounts.

In OpenERP, analytic accounts are linked to general accounts, but they are treated independently. So you can enter various different analytic operations that have no counterpart in the general financial accounts.

While the structure of the general chart of accounts is imposed by law, the analytic chart of accounts is built to fit a company's needs closely.

Just as in the general accounts, you will find accounting entries in the different analytic accounts. Each analytic entry can be linked to a general account, or not, as you wish. Conversely, an entry in a general account can be linked to one, several, or no corresponding analytic accounts.

You will discover many advantages of this independent representation below. For the more impatient, here are some of those advantages:

- you can manage many different analytic operations,

- you can modify an analytic plan on the fly, during the course of an activity, because of its independence,

- you can avoid an explosion in the number of general accounts,

- even those companies that do not use OpenERP's general accounts can use the analytic accounts for management.

Who Benefits from Analytic Accounts?

Unlike general accounts, analytic accounts in OpenERP are not so much an accounting tool for accountants as a management tool for everyone in the company. (That is why they are also called management accounts.)

The main users of analytic accounts should be the directors, general managers and project managers.

Analytic accounts make up a powerful tool that can be used in different ways. The trick is to create your own analytic structure for a chart of accounts that closely matches your company's needs.

To Each Enterprise its own Analytic Chart of

Accounts   10

To illustrate analytic accounts clearly, you will follow three use cases, each in one of three different types of company:

1. Industrial Manufacturing Enterprise,

2. Law Firm,

3. IT Services Company.

10.1 Case 1: Industrial Manufacturing Enterprise

In industry, you will often find analytic charts of accounts structured into departments and products the company itself is built on.

So the objective is to examine the costs, sales and margins by department and by product. The first level of the structure comprises the different departments, and the lower levels represent the product ranges the company makes and sells.

 Analytic Chart of Accounts for an Industrial Manufacturing Company

    1. Marketing Department

    2. Commercial Department

    3. Administration Department

    4. Production

        • Product Range 1

        • Sub-groups

        • Product Range 2

In daily use, it is useful to mark the analytic account on each purchase invoice. The analytic account is the one to which the costs of that purchase should be allocated. When the invoice is approved, it will automatically generate the entries for both the general and the corresponding analytic accounts. So, for each entry on the general accounts, there is at least one analytic entry that allocates costs to the department which incurred them.

Here is a possible breakdown of some general accounting entries for the example above, allocated to various analytic accounts:

Table 10.1: Breakdown of general and analytic accounting entries (Case 1)

General accounts				Analytic accounts	
Title	Account	Debit	Credit	Account	Value
Purchase of Raw Material	600	1500		Production / Range 1	-1 500
Subcontractors	602	450		Production / Range 2	-450
Credit Note for defective materials	600		200	Production / Range 1	200
Transport charges	613	450		Production / Range 1	-450
Staff costs	6201	10000		Marketing	-2 000
				Commercial	-3 000
				Administrative	-1 000
				Production / Range 1	-2 000
				Production / Range 2	-2 000
PR	614	450		Marketing	-450

The analytic representation by department enables you to investigate the costs allocated to each department in the company.

So, the analytic chart of accounts shows the distribution of the company's costs using the example above:

Table 10.2: Analytic chart of accounts (Case 1)

Account	Total
Marketing Department	-2 450
Commercial Department	-3 000
Administration Department	-1 000
Production	-6 200
Product Range 1	-3 750
Product Range 2	-2 450

In this example of a hierarchical structure in OpenERP, you can analyse not only the costs of each product range, but also the costs of the whole production. The balance of a summary account (*Production*) is the sum of the balances of the child accounts.

A report that relates both general accounts and analytic accounts enables you to get a breakdown of costs within a given department. An analysis of the Production / Product Range 1 department is shown in this table:

Table 10.3: Report merging both general and analytic accounts for a department (Case 1)

Production / Product Range 1	
General Account	Amount
600 – Raw Materials	- 1 300
613 – Transport charges	- 450
6201 – Staff costs	-2 000
Total	-3 750

The examples above are based on a breakdown of the costs of the company. Analytic allocations can be just as effective for sales. That gives you the profitability (sales - costs) of different departments.

Representation by Unique Product Range

This analytic representation by department and by product range is generally used by trading companies and industries.

A variant of this, is not to break it down by sales and marketing departments, but to assign each cost to its corresponding product range. This will give you an analysis of the profitability of each product range.

Choosing one over the other depends on how you look at your marketing effort. Is it a global cost allocated in some general way, or is each product range responsible for its own marketing costs?

10.2 Case 2: Law Firm

Law firms generally adopt management by case, where each case represents a current client file. All of the expenses and products are then attached to a given file.

A principal preoccupation of law firms is the invoicing of hours worked, and the profitability by case and by employee.

Mechanisms used for encoding the hours worked will be covered in detail in *Human Resources*. Like most system processes, hours worked are integrated into the analytic accounting. Every time an employee enters a timesheet for a number of hours, that automatically generates analytic accounts corresponding to the cost of those hours in the case concerned. The hourly charge is a function of the employee's salary. So a law firm will opt for an analytic representation which reflects the management of the time that employees work on the different client cases.

Example Representation of an Analytic Chart of Accounts for a Law Firm

1. Absences

    - Paid Absences
    - Unpaid Absences

2. Internal Projects

    - Administrative
    - Others

3. Client Cases

    - Client 1
        - Case 1.1
        - Case 1.2
    - Client 2
        - Case 2.1

All expenses and sales are then attached to a case. This gives the profitability of each case and, at a consolidated level, of each client.

Billing for the different cases is a bit unusual. The cases do not match any entry in the general account nor do they come from purchase or sales invoices. They are represented by the various analytic operations and do not have exact counterparts in the general accounts. They are calculated on the basis of the hourly cost per employee. These entries are automatically created when billing worksheets.

At the end of the month when you pay salaries and benefits, you integrate them into the general accounts but not in the analytic accounts, because they have already been accounted for in billing each account. A report that relates data from the analytic and general accounts then lets you compare the totals, so you can readjust your estimates of hourly cost per employee depending on the time actually worked.

The following table shows an example of different analytic entries that you can find for your analytic account:

Table 10.4: Analytic Entries for the Account Chart (Case 2)

Title	Account	Amount	General Account	Debit	Credit
Study the file (1 h)	Case 1.1	-15			
Search for information (3 h)	Case 1.1	-45			
Consultation (4 h)	Case 2.1	-60			
Service charges	Case 1.1	280	705 – Billing services		280
Stationery purchase	Administrative	-42	601 – Furniture purchase	42	
Fuel Cost -Client trip	Case 1.1	-35	613 – Transports	35	
Staff salaries			6201 – Salaries		3 000

Such a structure allows you to make a detailed study of the profitability of various transactions. In this example, the cost of Case 1.1 is 95.00 (the sum of the analytic costs of studying the files, searching for information and fuel costs), but has been invoiced at 280.00, which gives you a gross profit of 185.00.

But an interest in analytical accounts is not limited to a simple analysis of the profitability of different cases.

The same data can be used for automatic recharging of the services to the client at the end of the month. To invoice clients, just take the analytic costs in that month and apply a selling price factor to generate the invoice. Invoicing mechanisms for this are explained in greater detail in *Services & Project Management*. If the client requires details of the services used on the case, you can print the service entries in the analytic account for this case.

Invoicing Analytic Costs

Most software that manages billing enables you to recharge hours worked. In OpenERP, these services are automatically represented by analytic costs. But many other OpenERP documents can also generate analytic costs, such as credit notes and purchases of goods.

So when you invoice the client at the end of the month, it is possible for you to include all the analytic costs, and not just the hours worked. So, for example, you can easily recharge the whole cost of your journeys to the client.

10.3 Case 3: IT Services Company

Most IT service companies face the following problems:

- project planning,
- invoicing, profitability and financial follow-up of projects,
- managing support contracts.

To deal with these problems, you would use an analytic chart of accounts structured by project and by contract. A representation of that is given in the following example:

Example Analytic Representation of a Chart of Accounts for an IT Services Company

1. Internal Projects

    -   Administrative and Commercial
    -   Research and Development

2. Client Projects

    -   Client 1
        -   Project 1.1
        -   Project 1.2
    -   Client 2
        -   Project 2.1
        -   Project 2.2

3. Support Contracts – 20h

    -   Customer X
    -   Customer Y

The management of services, expenditures and sales is similar to that presented above for lawyers. Invoicing and the study of profitability are also similar.

But now look at support contracts. These contracts are usually limited to a prepaid number of hours. Each service posted in the analytic accounts shows the remaining hours of support. To manage support contracts, you would use the quantities and not the amounts in the analytic entries.

In OpenERP, each analytic line lists the number of units sold or used, as well as what you would usually find there – the amount in currency units (USD or GBP, or whatever other choice you make). So you can sum the quantities sold and used on each analytic account to determine whether any hours of the support contract remain. To differentiate services from other costs in the analytic account, you use the concept of the analytic journal. Analytic entries are then allocated into the different journals:

-   service journal,

-   expense journal,

-   sales journal,

-   purchase journal.

To obtain the detailed breakdown of a support contract, you only have to look at the service journal for the analytic account corresponding to the contract in question.

Finally, the analytic account can be used to forecast future needs. For example, monthly planning of staff on different projects can be seen as an analytic budget limited to the service journal. Accounting entries are expressed in quantities (such as number of hours, and numbers of products), and in amounts in units of currency (USD or GBP for instance).

So you can set up planning on just the basis of quantities. Analysing the analytic budget enables you to compare the budget (that is, your plan) to the services actually carried out by month end.

Cash Budgets

Problems of cash management are amongst the main difficulties encountered by small growing businesses. It is really difficult to predict the amount of cash that will be available when a company is young and rapidly growing.

If the company adopts management by case, then staff planning can be represented in the analytic accounts report, as you have seen.

But since you know your selling price for each of the different projects, you can see that it is easy to use the plan in the analytic accounts to more precisely forecast the amounts that you will invoice in the coming months.

.

Analytic Entries 11

11.1 Integrated with General Accounting

Just as in general accounting, analytic entries should be related to an account and an analytic journal.

Analytic records can be distinguished from general records by the following characteristics:

- they are not necessarily legal accounting documents,

- they do not necessarily belong to an existing accounting period,

- they are managed according to their date and not an accounting period,

- they do not generate both a debit and a credit entry, but a positive amount (income) or a negative amount (cost).

Figure 11.1: *Analytic Account Records for a Customer Project*

The figure *Analytic Account Records for a Customer Project* (page 79) represents the entries in an analytic account for a customer project.

You can see there:

- the service costs for staff working on the project,

- the costs for reimbursing the expenses of a return journey to the customer,

- purchases of goods that have been delivered to the customer,

- sales for recharging these costs.

11.2 Manual Entries

Even though most analytic entries are produced automatically by the other OpenERP documents, it is sometimes necessary to record manual entries. It is usually needed for certain analytic operations which have no counterpart in the general accounts.

To record manual entries, go to the menu *Accounting → Journal Entries → Analytic Journal Items* and click the *Create* button.

Analytic Entries

To make an analytic entry, OpenERP asks you to specify a general account. This is given only for information in the different cross-reports. It will not create any new entries in the general accounts.

Select a journal and complete the different fields. Write an expense as a negative amount and income as a positive amount.

Entering a Date

To enter a date in the editable list you can use the calendar widget in the web client or, in the GTK client, if you enter just the day of the month OpenERP automatically completes the month and year when you press the Tab key.

Example Cost Redistribution

One of the uses of manual data entry for analytic operations is reallocation of costs. For example, if a development has been done for a given project, but can be used again for another project, you can reallocate part of the cost to the other project.

In this case, make a positive entry on the first account and a negative entry for the same amount on the account of the second project.

11.3 Automated Entries

Analytic accounting is totally integrated with the other OpenERP modules, so you never have to re-enter the records. They are automatically generated by the following operations:

- confirmation of an invoice generates analytic entries for sales or purchases connected to the account shown in the invoice line,

- the entry of a service generates an analytic entry for the cost of this service to the given project,

- the manufacturing of a product generates an entry for the manufacturing cost of each operation in the product range.

Other documents linked to one of these three operations produce analytic records indirectly. For example, when you are entering a customer sales order, you can link it to the customer's analytic account. When you are managing by case or project, mark the project with that order. This order will then generate a customer invoice, which will be linked to the analytic account. When the invoice is validated, it will automatically create general and analytic accounting records for the corresponding project.

Expense receipts from an employee can be linked to an analytic account for reimbursement. When a receipt is approved by the company, a purchase invoice is created. This invoice represents a debit on the company in favour of the employee. Each line of the purchase invoice is then linked to an analytic account which automatically allocates the costs for that receipt to the corresponding project.

To visualise the general entries following these different actions, you can use one of the following menus:

1. To see all of the entries, *Accounting → Journal Entries → Analytic Journal Items*

2. To see the entries per account, per user, per product or per partner, you can use the menu *Accounting → Reporting → Statistic Reports → Analytic Entries Analysis*.

Figure 11.2: *Analytic Entries Analysis*

11.4 Analytic Models

Standard OpenERP allows you to post analytic entries to one chart at a time. Using the *Analytic Model* concept (install the option `Multiple Analytic Plans` from the *Add New Features* wizard), you can distribute your income or expenses to one or several analytic charts of account at the same time. You can define the combination of analytic plans through the menu *Accounting → Configuration → Analytic Accounting → Multi Plans → Analytic Plan*.

Figure 11.3: *Definition of Analytic Plan*

Using the link *Distribution Models* at the right side of the *Analytic Plan* form, you can define the distribution of either your expenses while creating a supplier invoice, or revenue when defining customer invoices. Thanks to these models, you can have one amount distributed amongst several analytic accounts. Models can be reused, and they can be applied to one analytic chart of accounts, but also to a combination of various charts of account, such as projects and cost centers.

Figure 11.4: *Definition of Distribution Models*

For example, when you create the invoice (suppose 1000 EUR) for the product `Client Project` with the analytic distribution defined above.

When the invoice has been validated, you can find the Analytic Journal Entries with the amount distributed amongst the analytic accounts through the menu *Accounting → Journal Entries → Analytic Journal Items*.

Figure 11.5: *Journal Entries with Distributed Amount*

You can also specify a default *Analytic Distribution* for a particular product, partner, user and company for a specific time interval using the menu *Accounting → Configuration → Analytic Accounting → Analytic Defaults*.

Part VI

Financial Analysis

This chapter is dedicated to statutory taxation and financial reporting from OpenERP. Whether you need reports about customers and suppliers, or statements for various statutory purposes, OpenERP enables you to carry out a whole range of parametric analyses regarding the financial health of your company.

Whether you want to analyse the general health of your company or review the status of an Account Receivable in detail, your company's accounts are the place to define your various business indicators.

To show you the most accurate picture of your business, OpenERP's accounting reports are flexible, and the results are calculated in real time. This enables you to automate recurring actions and to change your operations quickly when a company-wide problem (such as cash reserves dropping too low or receivables climbing too high) or a local problem (a customer that has not paid, or a project budget overspend) occurs.

This chapter describes the various reports and financial statements supplied by OpenERP's accounting modules. It also describes how OpenERP handles purchase and sales taxation, and the related tax reporting.

General Ledger and Trial Balance 12

A general ledger includes accounts with their debits and credits, and shows all transactions in an account, for one period, for several periods or for a financial year.

To print the *General Ledger*, you can use the menu *Accounting → Reporting → Legal Reports → Accounting Reports → General Ledger*. You will find the following wizard which is used to filter the resulting report.

Figure 12.1: *Preparing a General Ledger*

Select the proper options and journal(s) from the above wizard to print the *General Ledger*. The report can also be filtered by date or by period. When you choose to print the general ledger from one date to another, or for one or more periods, you can also have the initial balances printed for the periods preceding the periods you selected. You can sort the report by date or by journal / partner.

Figure 12.2: *General Ledger*

General Ledger for one or more accounts

When you want to print the general ledger for one or more accounts, go to the menu *Accounting* → *Configuration* -> *Financial Accounting* → *Accounts* → *Accounts*. Select the account(s) for which you want to print the general ledger and click the *General Ledger* report at the right side of the screen.

While the general ledger displays transactions for an account, a trial balance will show one amount (either debit or credit) for each account. The aim of the trial balance is to prove that the total of all debit balances is equal to the total of all credit balances.

To print the *Trial Balance*, go to the menu *Accounting* → *Reporting* → *Legal Reports* → *Accounting Reports* → *Trial Balance*. This report allows you to print or generate a PDF of your trial balance, allowing you to quickly check the balance of each of your accounts in a single report. A trial balance may include all accounts (even the ones without balance), only accounts with transactions or accounts of which the balance is not equal to zero. You can print a trial balance for all posted entries (meaning entries with a Valid state) or all entries, in which case the report will also print entries in a draft state. This option is useful, for instance, when your new financial year has just been opened, and you are preparing miscellaneous entries in the previous financial year.

Figure 12.3: *Trial Balance*

Reporting for One or More Accounts

You can print the *Trial Balance* report directly from the *Account* form too.

Balance Sheet and Profit & Loss Report 13

OpenERP also offers a Balance Sheet and a Profit & Loss Report.

A *Balance Sheet* is a financial statement that summarises the assets, liabilities and shareholders' equity of a company at a specific point in time. These three balance sheet segments give investors an idea as to what the company owns and owes, as well as the amount invested by the shareholders.

The balance sheet complies with the formula below:

Assets = Liabilities + Shareholders' Equity.

A balance sheet is often described as a snapshot of a company's financial condition.

The accounts displayed in the Balance Sheet are linked to an account type for which the P&L / Balance Sheet parameter is set to Balance Sheet (either Assets or Liabilities account). To configure *Account Types*, go to *Accounting → Configuration → Financial Accounting → Accounts → Account Types*.

The Balance Sheet can be printed from the menu *Accounting → Reporting → Legal Reports → Accounting Reports → Balance Sheet*. You can print this report in Landscape mode too.

Reserve & Profit and Loss Account

A Balance Sheet needs a reserve & profit and loss account, but instead of entering it each time you start the report, you can add a default Reserve & Profit and Loss account through the menu:menuselection:*Settings –> Companies –> Companies* on the Configuration tab. This account will be used as a counterpart to balance your accounts.

The *Profit & Loss Report* is a financial statement which gives a summary of the revenues, costs and expenses during a specific period of time. Such a report provides information that shows the ability of a company to generate profit by increasing revenue and reducing costs. The P&L statement is also known as an "Income Statement".

The purpose of the Profit & Loss Report is to show managers and accountants whether the company earned or lost money during the report period.

In general, the Profit and Loss report will be used to determine profit ratios, to examine sales prices and costs, and to set marketing budgets, for instance.

The accounts displayed in the Profit and Loss Report are linked to an account type for which the "P&L / Balance Sheet parameter is set to Profit & Loss (either Expense or Income account). To configure Account types, go to *Accounting → Configuration → Financial Accounting → Account Types*.

The Profit and Loss report can be printed from the menu *Accounting → Reporting → Legal Reports → Accounting Reports → Profit And Loss*.

Figure 13.1: *Profit and Loss Wizard*

Figure 13.2: *Profit and Loss Report*

The Accounting Journals 14

A journal allows you to list entries in chronological order (by default according to date). Each entry posted in OpenERP is recorded in such a journal. To configure the different accounting journals, go to the menu *Accounting → Configuration → Financial Accounting → Journals → Journals*.

Figure 14.1: *Defining a Journal*

OpenERP provides three main reports regarding the journals:

- To print a *Journal*, use the menu *Accounting → Reporting → Legal Reports → Journals → Journals*. This report will show all entries per journal, e.g. sales entries, purchase entries, etc. Each transaction is mentioned, with date, reference, document number, account, partner, description and debit and credit amount. The `Journal` report can be printed per period and per journal.

Journal

Chart of Accounts	Fiscal Year	Journal	Filters By	Entries Sorted By	Target Moves
Your Company	Fiscal Year 2011	Purchase Journal	No Filter	Date	All Posted Entries

Date	Ref	Move	Account	Partner	Label	Debit	Credit
08/2011	EXJ					968.00 €	968.00 €
08/01/2011	450	EXJ/2011/0003	612100	Distrib PC	Phone bill	800.00 €	0.00 €
08/01/2011	450	EXJ/2011/0003	411059	Distrib PC	VAT-IN-V82-21-5-C1 - VAT ..	168.00 €	0.00 €
08/01/2011	450	EXJ/2011/0003	440000	Distrib PC	/	0.00 €	968.00 €

Figure 14.2: *Printing a Journal*

- To print a *General Journal*, use the menu *Accounting → Reporting → Legal Reports → Journals → General Journals*. A General Journal will print a page per period for any journal entries posted in that period, and totalised per journal. The report will show the period, the journal, debit, credit and balance, but no details of the related entries.

General Journal

Chart of Accounts	Fiscal Year	Journals	Filter By	Target Moves
Your Company	Fiscal Year 2011	TSAJ, TSCNJ, TEXJ, TECNJ, TBNK, TCHK, TCSH, TMIS, TOEJ, STJ, SAJ, EXJ, SCNJ, ECNJ, MISC, BNK1, as	No Filter	All Posted Entries

Code	Journal Name	Debit	Credit	Balance
Total:		75039.88	76039.88	-1000.00 €
08/2011 :		2057.00	2057.00	0.00 €
EXJ	Purchase Journal	968.00	968.00	0.00 €
SAJ	Sales Journal	1089.00	1089.00	0.00 €

Figure 14.3: *Printing a General Journal*

- To print a *Centralizing Journal*, use the menu *Accounting → Reporting → Legal Reports → Journals → Centralizing Journal*. A centralizing journal gives a summary per account for each journal and period of debit, credit and balance.

Centralized Journal

Chart of Accounts	Fiscal Year	Journal	Filter By	Target Moves
Your Company	2011	Sales Journal	No Filter	All Posted Entries

A/C No.	Account Name	Debit	Credit	Balance
Total:		17920.94	17920.94	0.00 €
400000	Clients	17920.94	0.00	-17920.94 €
701000	Ventes en Belgique	0.00	17414.00	17414.00 €
451054	T.V.A. à payer	0.00	506.94	506.94 €

Figure 14.4: *Printing a Centralizing Journal*

Tax Declaration 15

Information required for a tax declaration is automatically generated by OpenERP from invoices. In the section on invoicing, you will have seen that you can get details of tax information from the area at the bottom left of an invoice.

You can also get the tax information when you open a journal entry by looking at the columns to the right of each line.

Figure 15.1: *Journal Entry with VAT Information*

OpenERP keeps a tax chart that you can reach from the menu *Accounting → Charts → Chart of Taxes*. The wizard will propose to display entries for the current period only, but you can also leave the period empty to see a complete financial year. The structure of the chart is for calculating the VAT declaration, but all the other taxes can be calculated as well (such as the French DEEE).

Tax Case Name	Case Code	Period Sum	Year Sum
▽ Opérations à la sortie	II	0.0	900.0
▷ Operations soumises à un régime particulier	II. A	0.0	0.0
▽ TVA due par le déclarant	II. B	0.0	900.0
Opérations avec TVA à 6%	01	0.0	0.0
Opérations avec TVA à 12%	02	0.0	0.0
Opérations avec TVA à 21%	03	0.0	900.0
▽ TVA etrangère due par le cocontractant	II. C	0.0	0.0
Services intra-communautaires	44	0.0	0.0
▽ Opérations avec TVA due par le cocontractant	II. D	0.0	0.0
Opérations avec TVA due par le cocontractant	45	0.0	0.0
▷ Livraisons intra-communautaire exemptées	II. E	0.0	0.0
▷ Autres opérations exemptées	II. F	0.0	0.0
▷ Notes de crédit délivrées et corrections négatives	II. C	0.0	0.0
▽ Opérations à l'entrée	III	57000.0	57800.0
▽ Opérations à l'entrée y compris notes de crédit et corrections	III. A	57000.0	57800.0
Marchandises, matières premières et auxiliaires	81	0.0	0.0
Services et biens divers	82	0.0	800.0
Biens d'investissement	83	57000.0	57000.0
▷ Notes de crédit reçues et corrections négatives	III. B	0.0	0.0
▷ Acquisition intra-communautaires et ventes ABC	III. C	0.0	0.0
▷ Autres opérations à l'entrée avec TVA due par le déclarant	III. D	0.0	0.0
▷ Services intracommunautaires avec report de perception	III. E	0.0	0.0
▽ Solde (71-72)	VI	-11970.0	-11949.0
▷ A payer - Total	XX	0.0	189.0
▷ A déduire - Total	YY	11970.0	12138.0
▷ Acompte	VII	0.0	0.0

Figure 15.2: *Example of a Belgian VAT Structure*

The tax chart represents the amount of each area of the VAT declaration for your country. It is presented in a hierarchical structure which lets you see the detail only of what interests you and hides the less interesting subtotals. This structure can be altered as you wish to fit your needs.

You can create several tax charts if your company is subject to different types of tax or tax-like accounts, such as:

- authors' rights,

- ecotaxes, such as the French DEEE for recycling electrical equipment.

By creating several charts of taxes, you can print different declarations from the menu *Accounting → Reporting → Generic Reporting → Taxes → Taxes Report*. Simply select the chart of taxes you want to print in the wizard.

Each accounting entry can then be linked to one of the tax accounts. This association is done automatically from the taxes which had previously been configured in the invoice lines.

Tax Declaration

Some accounting software manages the tax declaration in a dedicated general account. The declaration is then limited to the balance in the specified period. In OpenERP, you can create an independent chart of taxes, which has several advantages:

- it is possible to allocate only a part of the tax transaction,

- it is not necessary to manage several general accounts depending on the type of sales and the type of tax,

- you can restructure your chart of taxes as required.

At any time, you can check your chart of taxes for a given period using the report *Accounting → Reporting → Generic Reporting → Taxes → Taxes Report*.

Data is updated in real time. This is very useful because it enables you to preview at any time the tax that you owe at the start and end of the month or quarter.

Furthermore, for your tax declaration, you can click one of the tax accounts to investigate the detailed entries that make up the full amount. This helps you search for errors, such as when you have entered an invoice at full tax rate when it should have been zero-rated for an intracommunity trade or for charity.

Management Indicators

16

With OpenERP you can also create your own financial reports. This feature is now included in standard OpenERP. Go to *Accounting -_> Configuration → Financial Accounting → Financial Reports → Account Reports* and click `Create`.

Suppose we would like to create our company Balance Sheet. The first report to be created, should be a View report which will contain the final details. Keep the default Sequence 0.

Now create the `Assets` report, and set `Balance Sheet` as the parent for this report. Set the Sequence to 1.

Now create the `Liabilities` report, and set `Balance Sheet` as the parent for this report too. Set the Sequence to 2.

Both these reports are of the `View` type.

Apart from the `View` type, you can select three other types: `Accounts`, `Account Type` and `Report Value`.

- *Accounts*: here you can select view accounts or individual accounts that should be included in the report. View accounts offer the advantage that when new accounts are added as a child of such view account, they will automatically be printed on the report. When selecting individual accounts, you need to specifically add each newly created account to get the correct report.

- *Account Type*: selecting an account type means that all accounts related to the selected account type(s) will be printed on the report.

- *Report Value*: thanks to this value you can include the balance of existing reports in another report. Example: create a profit & loss report (view) including costs (account class 6) and income (account class 7). In the Balance Sheet, define a report Profit&Loss Balance, with Balance Sheet as the Parent. Set the type to Report Value and link it to the P&L view report you defined. This way, the balance sheet will print the Profit&Loss result.

Figure 16.1: *Financial Reports*

Create a report to print the Asset accounts (class 2 from the Belgian ledger) on the Assets side of the report. As a Parent, define the Assets report; sequence 3, type Accounts. If you want to use all accounts of class 2, just select the class (view account). You can also select various asset accounts. You could also have set this report to Account Type, with type Immo.

If you just want the sum of the selected accounts to appear, you leave the settings as they are. Should you wish to print the account details as well, you can select the `Display details` checkbox. The report will then also print the selected account numbers.

To print the results, go to *Accounting → Reporting → Legal Reports → Accounting Reports → Financial Report*. Select the report you want to print (only reports of the View type will be displayed in the list). You can also print a report for specific periods or dates. If you select the `Enable Comparison` checkbox, an extra `Comparison` tab will appear in which you can, for instance, select periods from a previous financial year. You have to give the comparison column a name through the `Column Label` field.

Balance Sheet

Chart of Accounts	Fiscal Year	Filter By
Your Company	2011	No Filter

Name	Balance
Assets	**0.00 €**
Asset	0.00 €
Liabilities	**-6200.00 €**
Capital	-6200.00 €
100000 Capital non amorti	-18550.00 €
101000 Capital non appelé	12350.00 €

Figure 16.2: *Example of a Financial Report*

Good Management Budgeting 17

Budgets are important for a company to get a good grip on forecasted expenses and revenues. They allow you to measure your actual financial performance against the planned one.

OpenERP manages its budgets using both General and Analytic Accounts. Go to *Settings → Modules → Modules* and install `account_budget` to be able to do this.

The first step in defining budgets is to determine the general accounts for which you want to keep budgets (typically expense or income accounts). That is what you will use `Budgetary Positions` for, from the menu *Accounting → Configuration → Budgets → Budgetary Positions*. Here you can select the general accounts for which you want to keep budgets. The aim is to group general accounts logically, according to sales or purchases, for instance. OpenERP has no limitations as to the account types that can be used for budgeting.

Figure 17.1: *Budgetary Position for Sales*

To define your budgets, go to the menu *Accounting → Budgets → Budgets*. Define a new budget by clicking the *New* button.

Figure 17.2: *Optimistic Budget*

Budget Revisions

Even though you *can* modify a budget at any time to make a revision, we recommend you to create a new budget, because otherwise you will have no history of changes.

Rather than edit an existing budget, make a new version so that you can keep your original estimates safe for comparison. This lets you analyse your changing perspectives of the company from revision to revision.

To define your budgets, start by entering a *Name*, a *Code*, a *Start Date* and an *End Date* for your new budget. Then you can define the budgeted amounts for each analytic account within a specified period, one by one (enter negative amounts for purchases, positive amounts for sales). For each, you define:

- an *Analytic Account*

- a *Budgetary Position*, for example `Sales` or `Purchases`,

- a *Start Date* and an *End Date* for the budget,

- a *Planned Amount* in the default currency of the chart of accounts.

Once this information is completed, save your budget.

A budget has various stages:

- *Confirmed*: the budget is to be reviewed, but it can still be changed before actual approval;

- *Approved*: the budget is approved by the budget holder; the name of the user approving the budget will be displayed in the `Validate User` field.

You can cancel a budget and reset it to draft for the two preceding steps.

- *Done*: the budget is fully approved and no changes will be allowed. You can no longer cancel the budget and reset it to draft.

The *Theoretical Amount* indicates the actual amount that might have been realised for the budget concerned according to the current date. When your budget is 1200 for 12 months, and today is the 30 October, the theoretical amount will be 1000, since this is the actual amount that could have been realised to date.

To print a budget and make calculations of expenditure through budget, use the menu *Accounting → Budgets → Budgets*. OpenERP then gives you a list of available budgets. Select one or more budgets and then click *Print Budgets* to create the report for each, in a date range of your choice.

The `Print Budget` report gives an overview of each analytic account included in your budget, according to the individual budgetary positions for that account. From the percentage and the comparison of planned (budgeted) and practical (actual) amounts, you have a good view on your situation.

From the same list of actions, you can also print the `Print Summary` report, which will give you a total per analytic account (without splitting by budgetary position).

Each of these reports can be printed from a specific date to a specific date. The End Date selected in the wizard determines how the theoretical amount will be calculated; if you select the last day of your financial year, the theoretical amount will be calculated as a function of that date (thus considering a complete financial year). Note that the theoretical amount will be zero when the *Paid Date* entered is equal to or greater than the *End Date* for the budget.

The percentage for a budget is calculated as follows: (practical amount / theoretical amount) x 100. This way you get a view on how much of the forecasted amount has been actually realised in your accounting.

The figure *Printing a Budget* (page 97) gives an example of a budget produced by OpenERP.

Budget

Analysis from	Budget	Currency
01/01/2011 to 12/10/2011	Budget 2011: Optimistic	EUR

Description	Theoretical Amt	Planned Amt	Practical Amt	Perc(%)
Consultancy	**950.00 €**	**950.00 €**	**1400.00 €**	**147.37%**
Purchases	-250.00 €	-250.00 €	0.00 €	-0.00%
Sales	1200.00 €	1200.00 €	1400.00 €	116.67%
Training	**0.00 €**	**375.00 €**	**0.00 €**	**0.00%**
Sales	0.00 €	375.00 €	0.00 €	0.00%
Seagate P2	**6692.31 €**	**9000.00 €**	**0.00 €**	**0.00%**
Purchases	-1000.00 €	-1000.00 €	0.00 €	-0.00%
Sales	7692.31 €	10000.00 €	0.00 €	0.00%
Seagate P1	**18000.00 €**	**18000.00 €**	**0.00 €**	**0.00%**
Purchases	-2000.00 €	-2000.00 €	0.00 €	-0.00%
Sales	20000.00 €	20000.00 €	0.00 €	0.00%
Total :	**25642.31 €**	**28325.00 €**	**1400.00 €**	**5.46%**

Figure 17.3: *Printing a Budget*

Budget

Analysis from	Budget	Currency
01/01/2011 to 12/10/2011	Budget 2011: Optimistic	EUR

Description	Theoretical Amt	Planned Amt	Practical Amt	Perc(%)
Consultancy	950.00 €	950.00 €	1400.00 €	147.37%
Training	0.00 €	375.00 €	0.00 €	0.00%
Seagate P2	6692.31 €	9000.00 €	0.00 €	0.00%
Seagate P1	18000.00 €	18000.00 €	0.00 €	0.00%
Total :	25642.31 €	28325.00 €	1400.00 €	5.46%

Figure 17.4: *Summarised Budget*

You could also use the menu *Accounting → Reporting → Generic Reporting → Budgets → Budget Lines*. This gives an analysis of each budget line.

From the menu *Accounting → Configuration → Budgets → Budgetary Positions*, you can print the budgets for an individual budgetary position. Open a budgetary position, and click the *Budget Lines* tab for a graphical representation of your budgetary position.

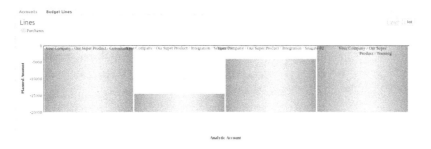

Figure 17.5: *Graphical Representation of Budgetary Position*

 Print Reports

You can also print budgets from the menu *Accounting → Configuration → Analytic Accounting → Analytic Accounts*.

The Accounting Dashboard 18

You can open the *Accounting Dashboard* in more than one way: either by clicking the `Accounting` button at the top of the web screen, or from the menu *Accounting → Reporting → Dashboard → Accounting Dashboard*.

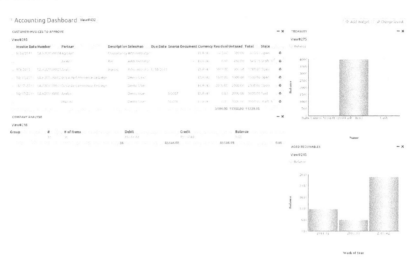

Figure 18.1: *Accounting Dashboard*

OpenERP gives you an accounting dashboard that will be presented to your accounting staff as they sign in to the Accounting system (you can also set the dashboard as their Home Page by setting the *Home Action* to `Accounting Dashboard` in the *User* form). This dashboard provides an analysis of the company's financial health at a glance.

The description of the different parts of the dashboard, from top to bottom, then from left to right, is as follows:

- *Customer Invoices to Approve* : gives the list of invoices waiting to be approved by an accountant.

- *Company Analysis* : lists the debit, credit and balance of all account types.

- *Treasury* : shows the balance per Bank account in graphical view.

- *Aged Receivables* : gives a weekly graph of the receivables that have not yet been reconciled.

For most of the panels of the *Accounting Dashboard*, you can click a line or a graph to investigate the detail of your financial indicators.

The *Accounting Dashboard* is dynamically integrated, which means that you can navigate easily through the data if you want more detail about certain factors, and edit the entries if necessary.

The `Change Layout` button at the top right allows you to change the way the dashboard is displayed; you can choose among several options, such as one column, two columns, etc. You can also add other features to the dashboard and customise it to your needs with the `Add  Widget` button. You can easily `Undo` changes or `Reset` the original dashboard.

Analytic Analysis 19

There are various reports designed for financial analysis based on the analytic accounts. Most of these reports are available directly from the tree of analytic accounts or from the form view of the analytic account.

From the *Accounting → Configuration → Analytic Accounting → Analytic Accounts* menu, select one or more analytic accounts and then click one of the reports in the *Reports* section at the right side of the screen. OpenERP provides the following financial analyses from the analytic accounts (and maybe more, depending on the additional installed modules):

- *Cost Ledger*,
- *Inverted Analytic Balance*,
- *Cost Ledger (only quantities)*,
- *Analytic Balance*,

 Menu

At the time of writing, there is no separate menu to print analytic reporting.

19.1 The Cost Ledger

The cost ledger provides the entries in general accounts for the selected analytic account(s). It enables you to make a detailed analysis of each operation carried out on one or several projects.

Cost Ledger

	Period from	Period to		Printing date	
	01/01/2011	10/24/2011		10/24/2011 12:32:13	

Date/Code	J.C. /Move name	Debit	Credit	Balance
Total:		500.00	0.00	500.00 €
4	Your Company / Our Super Product / Consultancy	500.00	0.00	500.00 €
700000	Ventes en Belgique	500.00	0.00	500.00 €
08/16/2011	Consultancy	500.00	0.00	500.00 €

Figure 19.1: *Cost Ledger*

19.2 Inverted Analytic Balance

The inverted analytic balance provides a summary report relating general accounts and analytic accounts. This report shows the balances of the general accounts broken down by the selected analytic accounts from date / to date.

Inverted Analytic Balance - EUR

Code	Name	Debit	Credit	Balance	Quantity
Total		500.00	0.00	500.00 €	1.00
700000	Ventes en Belgique	500.00	0.00	500.00 €	1.00
4	Your Company / Our Super Product / Consultancy	500.00	0.00	500.00 €	1.00

Figure 19.2: *Inverted Analytic Balance*

This enables you to analyse your costs by general account. For example, if you examine your general account for staff salaries, you can obtain all your salary costs broken down by the different analytic (or project) accounts.

19.3 The Cost Ledger (Quantities Only)

This report gives the details of entries for an analytic account and a list of selected journals. Only quantities are reported for this analysis, not costs and revenues. In the wizard you can select from period and to period and one or more journals.

Cost Ledger

Period from	Period to	Printing date
01/01/2011	10/25/2011	10/25/2011 09:59:56

Code/Date J.C./Move name	Quantity	Total
Total:		1.00
1 Your Company / Our Super Product / Integration / Seagate P1	Max Qty: 0.00	1.00
600000 Achats de matières premières		1.00
10/03/2011 PUR Purchase		1.00

Figure 19.3: *Cost Ledger with Quantities Only*

The report is often used to print the number of hours worked on a project, without exposing the costs and revenues. So you can show it to a customer as a record of the hours worked on a particular project.

To restrict the report to hours worked, without including sales and purchases, select only the services journal in the printing options.

Multiple Printing

To print several analytic accounts at once, you can make a multiple selection on the different accounts in the tree of accounts. Then click the appropriate *Report* in the toolbar (in the web client), or select one of the *Print* reports (in the GTK client), to export the whole selection into a single PDF document.

19.4 Analytic Balance

The analytic balance is a summary report that relates the analytic accounts to the general accounts. It shows the balances of the analytic accounts broken down by general account for a selected period. The analytic balance allows you to display a breakdown of each project by operation in the general accounts. Quantities are printed too. You can choose to include accounts without a balance as well.

When you select the analytic chart itself (the main analytic account), you can print the analytic balance for the entire analytic chart of accounts.

Analytic Balance - EUR

Code	Account Name	Debit	Credit	Balance	Quantity
Total		500.00	1500.00	-1000.00 €	2.00
4	Your Company / Our Super Product / Consultancy	500.00	0.00	500.00 €	1.00
700000	Ventes en Belgique	500.00	0.00	500.00 €	1.00
integration	Your Company / Our Super Product / Integration	0.00	1500.00	-1500.00 €	1.00
600000	Achats de matières premières	0.00	1500.00	-1500.00 €	1.00
1	Your Company / Our Super Product / Integration / Seagate P1	0.00	1500.00	-1500.00 €	1.00
600000	Achats de matières premières	0.00	1500.00	-1500.00 €	1.00
100	Your Company / Our Super Product	500.00	1500.00	-1000.00 €	2.00
600000	Achats de matières premières	0.00	1500.00	-1500.00 €	1.00
700000	Ventes en Belgique	500.00	0.00	500.00 €	1.00

Figure 19.4: *Analytic Balance*

This report gives you the profitability of a project for the different operations that you used to carry out the project.

Multi-company

In a multi-company environment, each company can have its own general chart of accounts on the same database. The two general charts of accounts are independent, but can be linked in a third chart using a view account to do the consolidation.

If the different companies collaborate on joint projects, they may all share the same analytic chart of accounts. In this environment, the cross-related reports like the balance and inverted balance are extremely useful, because they enable you to make an analysis per company by linking up to the general accounts.

19.5 Analytic Journals

From the *Accounting → Configuration → Analytic Accounting → Analytic Journals*, select one or more analytic journals and click the `Analytic Journal` report at the right side of the screen. This prints a report per analytic journal from debit and credit (general account versus analytic account).

Analytic Journal

Period from	Period to	Currency
01/01/2011	10/25/2011	EUR

Date	Code	Move Name	Account n°	General	Analytic
- Sales				**-500.00**	**500.00**
		Consultancy KI	700000 Ventes en Belgique	-500.00	
08/16/2011		Consultancy	4 - Consultancy		500.00

Figure 19.5: *Analytic Sales Journal*

19.6 Analytic Entries Analysis

You can have the statistical analysis on all analytic entries from the menu *Accounting → Reporting → Statistic Reports → Analytic Entries Analysis*. By default, analytic entries are grouped by analytic account and month, but you have many options to sort and regroup analytic entries. You can, for instance, first group the information by general account, then by analytic account.

Figure 19.6: *Statistical Report for Analytic Entries*

Graph

You can easily turn this analysis screen into a graph by clicking the *Graph* button at the top of the screen.

Part VII

An Introduction to Multicurrency Principles

As from version 6.1, OpenERP went through some changes regarding Multicurrency Management.

- Exchange differences are managed automatically by the reconciliation system, but no longer through the Write-Off part of the voucher.

- The payment voucher (which is also the reconciliation form of a bank statement) has been changed too. It now handles both the Exchange Difference and the Write-Off. The write-off is computed at the end of the payment voucher in order to reflect the difference between the payment and the amount allocated on invoices.

- The exchange difference is computed per line of invoice allocation and computed at the total reconciliation. So a payment for 3 invoices can have 3 journal entries generated for the exchange difference. The exchange difference is computed in order to reflect the change in the currency between the invoice entries and the payment entries.

Some examples of what can be accomplished in OpenERP.

Suppose your company is managed in EUR. If you invoice 500 USD to a customer (= 350 EUR at the date) and the receivable account is managed in USD, it means your customer owes you 500 USD (not 350 EUR). If the customer pays 400 CHF (= 200 EUR = 380 USD at that date), his credit is decreased by 380 USD, so he owes you 120 USD (which may be 83 EUR today).

An opposite example: suppose your company is managed in EUR. If you invoice 500 USD to a customer (= 350 EUR at the date) and the receivable account is managed in EUR (not in USD like above), it means your customer owes you 350 EUR (not 500 USD). If he pays 400 CHF (= 200 EUR = 380 USD at that date), his credit is decreased by 200 EUR, so he owes you 150 EUR (which may be 200 USD today).

 Currencies

In our examples, we start from the idea that you have a dedicated company account in foreign currency, related to a bank journal in the same foreign currency.

Getting Started with Multicurrency 20

OpenERP will now distinguish between exchange rate differences and write-off differences. To automatically register exchange differences, go to *Settings → Companies → Companies*, open your company and go to the `Configuration` tab. Add accounts for incoming and outgoing exchange rate differences. These will be used when making multi-currency entries.

20.1 Receivable Account in Currency

A partner can have invoices on several Receivable accounts, which is useful if you invoice him in different currencies. Please keep in mind that a partner can have one default receivable account defined in the `Customer` form. However, you are still allowed to use several receivable accounts for a customer, according to the currencies in which you invoice him. A partner can have invoices on several Receivable accounts, which is useful if you invoice him in different currencies. Please keep in mind that a partner can have one default receivable account defined in the Customer form. However, you are still allowed to use several receivable accounts for a customer, according to the currencies in which you invoice him.

When setting a secondary currency for an account, please think about the meaning of the *Secondary Currency* field in the `Account` form:

1. **Empty**: the account is managed in the currency of the company. This account can have journal items in currencies for information purposes, but all reports, such as the charts of accounts, use the currency of the company to compute account balances.

2. **Company Currency**: this means entries in other currencies than the company currency will not be accepted for this account. For example, suppose EUR is your company currency. You will not be able to invoice in USD if the receivable account has EUR as a secondary currency (if it is empty, you can).

3. **Foreign Currency**: if you select a secondary currency different from the company currency, OpenERP will consider this account as a multi-currency account. Every journal item will have a secondary amount in this currency; the secondary currency is required in this case. You can specify a foreign currency for bank accounts that you keep in a currency different from your company currency.

Figure 20.1: *Receivable Account in CHF*

20.2 Bank Account in Currency

A company can have several bank accounts, either in company currency (account which may perfectly well accept foreign currencies) or accounts in foreign currency. You can use the `Set up your Bank Accounts` wizard to easily create company banks, as well as the corresponding bank account and bank journal in one go. Go to the menu *Accounting → Configuration → Financial Accounting → Accounts → Setup your Bank Accounts*.

Bank Journal and Bank Account in Currency

Remember that the bank journal and its related bank account should be expressed in the same currency. OpenERP will display a message if you break this rule.

In this screen, specify your account number (either in normal or IBAN format) and select whether this account number has to be printed on reports. Select (or create) the bank name (containing also information related to your bank, such as name, address, BIC). In the example below we choose `Reserve`, the bank from the demo data. You can complete the address data if you have not updated your company's address yet. When you click the `Save` button, a financial `Account Journal` and a `Bank Account` will automatically be created.

Figure 20.2: *Defining a Bank Account in EUR*

Bank and BIC

When you create a new bank from the Company Bank Accounts screen and you enter the BIC (Bank Identifier Code) number, the Bank Name and Bank Identifier Code field will automatically be completed according to the data set for the bank. E.g. create a new bank KBC and add BIC KREDBEBB.

Bank Journal & Account

The bank account that is automatically created on Save wil be created in the company currency. If your bank account only allows a specific currency, such as CHF, you can easily change this from the `Set up your Bank Accounts` screen. Simply click the button at the right side of the `Account Journal` field, then select `Open`. Now open the `Default Debit Account` (or Credit, refers to the same bank account) in the same way and set the currency to CHF (see also the screen below). Remember to also change the `Account Type` of the bank account to "Financier". Add the currency CHF also to the Bank Journal itself.

Figure 20.3: *Defining a Bank Account*

Instead of using the `Set up your Bank Accounts` wizard, you can also create the bank account from the menu *Accounting → Configuration → Financial Accounting → Accounts*. Click `Accounts` to open the list of accounts.

Figure 20.4: *Defining a Bank Account in CHF*

In the following example we will use a Bank Journal in CHF with a bank account in the same currency. If such a journal does not exist yet, you can easily define one through the `Setup your Bank Accounts` wizard as explained before. Or you can create a bank journal from the menu *Accounting → Configuration → Financial Accounting → Journals → Journals*.

Figure 20.5: *Company Bank Account in CHF*

 Multi-currency View

When defining your journal, make sure to select the corresponding
`Display Mode`, i.e. **Bank/Cash Journal (Multi-Currency) View**.

Figure 20.6: *Bank Journal in CHF with Multicurrency View*

Creating an Invoice in CHF 21

21.1 Defining a Receivable Account for CHF

Go to the menu *Accounting → Configuration → Financial Accounting → Accounts* to create a new receivable account for your company.

Click `Create` to create a receivable account in CHF. This means that every entry posted to this receivable account, will need an amount expressed in CHF too.

Figure 21.1: *Defining an Account in CHF*

> **Duplicating**
>
> Note that you can also duplicate an existing receivable account. A quick way is to click the *Receivable Accounts* and then open the existing account. To duplicate this account, make sure the account is not in `Edit` mode. Click the `Cancel` button at the top of the account screen to display the *Duplicate* button.

Once this account has been defined, you can link it to the corresponding partner. Here we select partner `CamptoCamp`. On the `Accounting` tab of the `Customers` form, link the new Account Receivable in CHF. Notice that this is a default receivable account for this customer. In case you need to invoice him in a different currency, you can change the account receivable from the invoice.

21.2 Creating the Invoice

Before creating the invoice, make sure to check whether the correct rate has been defined. Go to the menu *Accounting → Configuration → Miscellaneous → Currencies* and open currency CHF. The rate defined to be valid as from 01/01/2011 (through the demo data) is 1.308600. Click Create, change the date to 11/01/2011 and add the rate 1.22530.

Currency Position

As from this version, you can also choose where to print the currency symbol through the `Symbol Position` field, either Before or After the amount.

Go to the menu *Accounting* → *Customers* → *Customer Invoices* anc click `Create` to create a new invoice for Camptocamp.

Select customer *Camptocamp*. Then change the currency of the invoice to CHF by clicking the *Change* button at the right side of the `Currency` field. Set the invoice date to the beginning of November, e.g. 3 November. This will allow us to show the exchange rate differences.

Currency

You can also create specific pricelists in the currency of the customer to not have to change the currency.

Sell a basic PC [PC1] to this customer and change the price to 500. Notice that the EUR price of Basic PC is automatically converted to CHF according to the valid rate (450 EUR * 1.225300 = 551.38 CHF). Click `Save & Close` to save the invoice line.

Confirm the invoice by clicking the `Validate` button.

Now you can immediately check what your journal entry looks like. Go to the `Other Info` tab and click the button next to the `Journal Entry` field, then click `Open` to see the entry and stay in the `Invoice` screen, or click `Journal Items` to go the list of entry lines. Now have a look at the journal items posted for this invoice. Notice that 500 CHF is automatically converted to 408.06 EUR, according to the exchange rate of 1.225300.

Encoding Payments 22

The customer pays you 200 CHF in advance on 12/01/2011. Your bank account in CHF will show an amount of 200 CHF with a counterpart in EUR at a rate of 1.4, i.e. 142.86 EUR. Before encoding this advance payment, you can update the exchange rate defined for CHF. Of course, you can also enter the correct amount in EUR from your statement. Go to the menu *Accounting → Configuration → Miscellaneous → Currencies* and open currency CHF. Click Create, change the date to 12/01/2011 and add the rate 1.4.

22.1 Paying an Advance

Camptocamp pays you 200 CHF (or 142.86 according to the exchange rate of 1.4) in advance. Go to the menu *Accounting → Journal Entries → Journal Items*. Select the bank journal you created (e.g. Reserve), enter the Period in which you want to post and click create to enter the advance payment.

Enter the payment as specified in the screenshot. Remember to change the date to 12/01. Start by entering the entry to the customer's receivable account. Make sure to enter a credit amount for the payment. In case you did not change the exchange rate, you can enter the EUR amount as recorded in your bank statement.

Press the Enter key when the first line is complete. Click the Save button at the end of the line to confirm the payment line.

Figure 22.1: *Registering an Advance Payment*

As you will notice, the entry has no number yet. The `Valid` status only indicates that the journal items are balanced.

You can confirm entries in various ways. usually, you will not confirm entries one by one, but in batch. To definitely post a batch of entries is, go to the menu *Accounting → Periodical Processing → Draft Entries → Post Journal Entries*. Here you can approve entries per journal and financial period.

You can also approve entries directly from the `Journal Items` view or the `Journal Entries` view.

22.2 Reporting and Follow-ups

To check your open entries for your customers, go to the *Accounting → Reporting → Generic Reporting → Partners* menu, select the `Partner Ledger` and tick the *With Currency* checkbox to also print the amounts in foreign currency.

Partner Ledger

Chart of Accounts	Fiscal Year	Journals	Filters By	Partner's	Target Moves
Your Company	Fiscal Year X 2011	TSAJ, TSCNJ, TEXJ, TECNJ, TBNK, TCHK, TCSH, TMIS, TOEJ, SAJ, EXJ, SCNJ, ECNJ, MISC, BNK1, BNK2	No Filter	Receivable Accounts	All Posted Entries

Date	JRNL	Ref	Account	Entry Label	Debit	Credit	Balance	Currency
- Camptocamp					408.06	142.86	265.20 €	
11/03/2011	SAJ	SAJ/2011/0001	400100	SAJ20... - /	408.06	0.00	408.06 €	500.00 CHF
12/01/2011	BNK2	BNK2/2011/0001	400100	- Adva...	0.00	142.86	265.20 €	200.00 CHF

Figure 22.2: *Partner Ledger with Currency*

From the *Customers* view, open customer `Camptocamp` and print the *Overdue Payments* report from the list of actions to see the customer statement.

You can send reminders as explained in this book as well.

22.3 Customer Pays the Remaining Amount

The statement you receive from your bank shows a payment of 300 CHF from your customer Camptocamp. The outstanding balance in company currency is 265.20 EUR. The amount in EUR that is on your bank statement, however, is 242.35 EUR (according to the new rate of 1.237900).

Go to the menu *Accounting → Customers → Customer Payment* and create a new payment for customer `Camptocamp`. Make sure to select the correct *Payment Method*, i.e. your bank journal, in our example the CHF bank journal.

Enter the amount of 300 CHF in the *Paid Amount* field and consider the advance payment and the 300 CHF payment as completely reconciled against the 500 CHF invoice.

Do not confirm, but simply check what it looks like. This way, we can show you another example which is a bit more complicated.

Figure 22.3: *Fully Reconciled Invoice*

22.4 Write-off and Exchange Rate

Now register a customer payment for the same customer Camptocamp. Enter a Paid Amount of 299 CHF (this is 1 CHF less than what the customer owes you). Notice that the advance payment is automatically considered as fully reconciled (second part of the screen). In the invoice part, you will see the invoice of 500 CHF, which is not considered as fully reconciled, but shows the Allocation amount of 499 CHF (299 of the payment plus the 200 CHF of the advance payment).

In this example we want to consider the invoice as fully paid, so check the *Full Reconcile*. Notice that the amount is automatically set to 500. Select the *Payment Difference* `Reconcile Payment Balance` and select a *Counterpart Account*.

Figure 22.4: *Reconciliation through Bank Statement with Exchange Difference and Write-off*

Of course, another example could be full payment by the customer, so no need to do a write-off, but only an entry for the exchange differences.

Figure 22.5: *Reconciliation through Bank Statement with Exchange Difference*

Part VIII

Managing your Assets

Easily manage your assets with OpenERP. This module is fully integrated with the financial and analytic accounting modules for a maximum of power. Manage the assets owned by your company and keep track of depreciation occurred on those assets. Of course, the system also allows you to create accounting moves of the depreciation lines.

Asset Management in OpenERP allows you to:

- Have different depreciation methods,

- Compute the depreciation according to the time period and the depreciation method specified,

- Keep track of all accounting entries based on the value,

- Have a fully integrated system with the financial and analytic accounting modules,

- Track changes on assets from any document in OpenERP.

You can manage your assets and the related accounting entries with the `account_asset` module.

From the menu *Accounting → Assets → Assets* you can store all information related to your assets. How much will be depreciated, what will be the depreciation amount based on the selected depreciation method, what is the date on which the asset is purchased, the purchase value of the asset, the supplier of the asset, etc.

You can also see different states of assets. If the asset is confirmed, the depreciation lines may be posted in the accounting system. An asset can be closed manually when depreciation is over or it will be closed automatically when the last depreciation line is posted.

The asset hierarchy is shown through the menu *Accounting → Assets → Asset Hierarchy*.

Statistical reporting about assets can be called from the menu *Accounting → Reporting → Statistic Reports → Assets Analysis*.

Depreciation Methods 23

The linear, or straight-line depreciation in the words of Wikipedia: <http://en.wikipedia.org/wiki/Depreciation#Straight-line_depreciation>

> Straight-line depreciation is the simplest and most-often-used technique, in which the company estimates the salvage value of the asset at the end of the period during which it will be used to generate revenues (useful life) and will expense a portion of original cost in equal increments over that period. The salvage value is an estimate of the value of the asset at the time it will be sold or disposed of; it may be zero or even negative. Salvage value is also known as scrap value or residual value.
>
> **Straight-line method:** (Annual Depreciation Expense = Cost of Fixed Asset - Residual Value) / Useful Life of Asset (years)
>
> For example, a vehicle that depreciates over 5 years, is purchased at a cost of € 17,000, and will have a salvage value of € 2000, will depreciate at € 3,000 per year: (€ 17,000 € 2,000) / 5 years = € 3,000 annual straight-line depreciation expense. In other words, it is the depreciable cost of the asset divided by the number of years of its useful life.
>
> This table illustrates the straight-line method of depreciation. Book value at the beginning of the first year of depreciation is the original cost of the asset. At any time book value equals original cost minus accumulated depreciation.
>
> **book value = original cost - accumulated depreciation** Book value at the end of year becomes book value at the beginning of next year. The asset is depreciated until the book value equals scrap value.
>
> If the vehicle were to be sold and the sales price exceeded the depreciated value (net book value) then the excess would be considered a gain and subject to depreciation recapture. In addition, this gain above the depreciated value would be recognized as ordinary income by the tax office. If the sales price is ever less than the book value, the resulting capital loss is tax deductible. If the sales price were ever more than the original book value, then the gain above the original book value is recognized as a capital gain.
>
> If a company chooses to depreciate an asset at a different rate from that used by the tax office then this generates a timing difference in the income statement due to the difference (at a point in time) between the taxation department's and company's view of the profit.

The degressive, or declining-balance depreciation method in the words of Wikipedia: <http://en.wikipedia.org/wiki/Depreciation#Straight-line_depreciation>

> Depreciation methods that provide for a higher depreciation charge in the first year of an asset's life and gradually decreasing charges in subsequent years are called accelerated depreciation methods. This may be a more realistic reflection of an asset's actual expected benefit from the use of the asset: many assets are most useful when they are new. One popular accelerated method is the *declining-balance method*. Under this method the book value is multiplied by a fixed rate.

Annual Depreciation = Depreciation Rate x Book Value at Beginning of Year

The most common rate used is double the straight-line rate. For this reason, this technique is referred to as the double-declining-balance method. To illustrate, suppose a business has an asset with € 1,000 original cost, € 100 salvage value, and 5 years useful life. First, calculate straight-line depreciation rate. Since the asset has 5 years useful life, the straight-line depreciation rate equals (100% / 5) 20% per year. With double-declining-balance method, as the name suggests, double that rate, or 40% depreciation rate is used.

When using the double-declining-balance method, the salvage value is not considered in determining the annual depreciation, but the book value of the asset being depreciated is never brought below its salvage value, regardless of the method used. The process continues until the salvage value or the end of the asset's useful life, is reached. In the last year of depreciation a subtraction might be needed in order to prevent book value from falling below estimated Scrap Value.

From double-declining to straight-line depreciation

Since double-declining-balance depreciation does not always depreciate an asset fully by its end of life, some methods also compute a straight-line depreciation each year, and apply the greater of the two. This has the effect of converting from declining-balance depreciation to straight-line depreciation at a midpoint in the asset's life. This is the way degressive depreciations are handled in Belgium and in France, for instance. Note that this method is not implemented in OpenERP.

Asset Categories

24

Asset categories contain the general accounting information and default depreciation rules for assets. They can be used as defined, but you can also adapt a defined category in case you need slightly different depreciation rules. You can create asset categories from the menu *Accounting → Configuration → Financial Accounting → Assets → Asset Categories*. Then click the `Create` button. Asset categories should represent the generally used depreciation rules in your company.

You can configure the following information:

- *Name*: A name for the asset category, e.g. machinery, office equipment, vehicles.

- *Journal*: A journal to store the accounting entries, typically a miscellaneous journal.

- *Asset Account*: This account holds the purchase value and will be credited when depreciation line is posted. For Belgium, e.g. 241000 Cars.

- *Depreciation Account*: Account, can be the same as the Asset Account or it can be different for storing depreciation separately. For Belgium, e.g. 241900 Depreciations on Cars.

- *Depr. Expense Account*: Expense account which will be debited when the depreciation line is posted, e.g. for Belgium 630100.

- *Time Method*: this method determines how the dates and the number of depreciations will be computed. There are two options: `Number of Depreciations` or `Ending Date`. According to the option selected, the following fields will be different.

  - Time Method *Number of Depreciations* You have to specify the number of times the goods will be depreciated, e.g. 5 years or 60 months, in the `Number of Depreciations` field. You als have to indicate the `Period Length`, meaning the number of times in 1 year you will post a depreciation entry (so, the duration in months between two depreciations). If you set this value to 1, for instance, OpenERP will create 12 entries in one year (one entry each month). If you set this to 12, OpenERP will create a single depreciation entry each year.

  - Time Method *Ending Date* You als have to indicate the `Period Length`, meaning the number of times in 1 year you will post a depreciation entry (so, the duration in months between two depreciations). If you set this value to 1, for instance, OpenERP will create 12 entries in one year. If you set this to 12, OpenERP will create a single depreciation entry each year. You should specify the `Ending Date` for the depreciation. Depreciations will not go beyond this date.

- *Computation Method* : Either `Linear` (Straight-line method of depreciation) or `Degressive` (declining-balance). See above for more information. When you select `Degressive`, the following field will be added.

  - *Degressive Factor* : If computation method is `Degressive`, you have to specify the degressive factor (i.e. the % used for declining-balance depreciation, e.g. 40%).

- *Prorata Temporis* : If checked, the first depreciation entry will be calculated from the purchase date, instead of the first day of your fiscal year. Example: a company with a fiscal year from 01/01 to 31/12 buys a car 20 December. With the pro rata temporis method, this car can be depreciated only for 12/365 during the first year.

- *Skip Draft State* : If the checkbox is selected, assets of this category will automatically be confirmed when created from an invoice. If you do not select this checkbox, you will have to confirm the asset before depreciation will start.

- *Analytic Account* allows you to add an analytic account to keep track of your assets.

We suggest you to create asset categories for each type of asset you will have in your company. Some examples: office equipment, buildings, vehicles. For each asset category, you can specify the depreciation method concerned. This allows you to automatically select the correct depreciation method when posting purchase invoices for assets, simply by selecting the corresponding asset category.

Figure 24.1: *Defining an Asset Category*

Registering Assets

25

The most common way to create assets is from a purchase invoice. From the *Accounting* → *Suppliers* → *Supplier Invoices* menu, click *Create* to create a supplier invoice. In the *Invoice line* you can click the *Create* button and enter the relevant data. Post the entry to corresponding asset account (such as 241000 for cars) and select the corresponding *Asset Category* in which you want to create this asset.

When you *Approve* the invoice, an asset will be created for the selected invoice line. You can see it by going to the menu *Accounting* → *Assets* → *Assets*.

Of course, you can create an asset directly from the menu *Accounting* → *Assets* → *Assets* and click *Create*. This is useful when you want to register historical assets. You can enter or look up the following information for assets.

- *Asset*: A name for the asset.

- *Asset Category*: Select a category for the asset to determine the depreciation method.

- *Reference*: optional field to specify an extra reference for the asset, e.g. the licence plate of a car. When the asset is created from a purchase invoice, by default this field will contain the invoice number.

- *Gross Value*: Gross purchase amount of the asset (including any non-reclaimable VAT).

- *Salvage Value*: the remaining value of an asset after it has been fully depreciated (also called remaining value).

- *Residual Value*: the actual amount left to be depreciated (by default the gross value - the salvage value, but updated according to depreciations posted).

The *General* tab contains the following information:

- *Parent Asset*: this box allows you to relate one asset to another one, e.g. if you buy a car kit for a car that is already an asset in your company.

- *Purchase Date*: Date on which the asset has been purchased.

- *Partner*: Supplier of the asset.

The default depreciation method from the asset category will be proposed, but it can be changed for an individual asset as long as the asset has not been confirmed.

On the *Depreciation board* tab, you can compute the depreciation again (e.g. if you changed the depreciation rules). Here will you see the depreciation table, based on the selected depreciation method and period. You can manually change the depreciation table by clicking the line concerned, for instance in case of rounding differences. Then you can confirm the asset by clicking the *Confirm Asset* button. The state of the asset will now be `Running`.

For confirmed assets, you can post the depreciation lines by clicking the *Create Move* button in a depreciation line. You can also see that the *Depreciation Amount* from a posted depreciation line will be deducted from the *Residual Value*. Of course, you do not have to post each asset individually. From the menu :menuselection:´Accounting –> Periodical Processing –> Recurring Entries –> Compute Assets´ you can post all assets for a specific period.

Asset Journal

According to the definition of the Asset Journal, entries may still be in draft status and require to be posted.

You can see the accounting entry for the posted depreciation lines on the *History* tab.

Figure 25.1: *Defining an Asset*

Depreciation Lines

Depreciation Date	Amount Already Depreciated	Depreciation Amount	Amount to Depreciate	P
2011-01-01	0.00	19945.21	380054.79	
2012-01-01	19945.21	20000.00	360054.79	
2013-01-01	39945.21	20000.00	340054.79	
2014-01-01	59945.21	20000.00	320054.79	
2015-01-01	79945.21	20000.00	300054.79	
2016-01-01	99945.21	20000.00	280054.79	
2017-01-01	119945.21	20000.00	260054.79	
2018-01-01	139945.21	20000.00	240054.79	
2019-01-01	159945.21	20000.00	220054.79	
2020-01-01	179945.21	20000.00	200054.79	
2021-01-01	199945.21	20000.00	180054.79	
2022-01-01	219945.21	20000.00	160054.79	
2023-01-01	239945.21	20000.00	140054.79	
2024-01-01	259945.21	20000.00	120054.79	
2025-01-01	279945.21	20000.00	100054.79	
2026-01-01	299945.21	20000.00	80054.79	
2027-01-01	319945.21	20000.00	60054.79	
2028-01-01	339945.21	20000.00	40054.79	
2029-01-01	359945.21	20000.00	20054.79	
2030-01-01	379945.21	20000.00	54.79	
2031-01-01	399945.21	54.79	0.00	

Figure 25.2: *The Depreciation Board*

Analysis of Assets 26

You can get a good view on your asset entries in several reports through the menu *Accounting →
Reporting → Legal reports → Accounting Reports*. You can run the *Trial Balance*, the *General Ledger*
or the *Balance Sheet*.

The *Accounting → Reporting → Statistic Reports → Assets Analysis* will give you the statistical report
of assets. This report is enhanced by various filters and groupings to assist you in your search for the
required information.

Part IX

Configuring Accounts from A to Z

Accounts have be configured to meet your company's needs. This chapter explains how to modify your chart of accounts, journals, access rights, initial account balances and default values for the initial configuration of your OpenERP accounts.

Good accounting software requires great usability and simplicity of data entry, as well as flexibility in configuring its different components. You should be able to easily modify the accounting module to meet your own needs, so that you can optimise it for the way you want to use it.

OpenERP lets you adapt and reconfigure many functions to ease the task of data entry:

- adding controls for data entry,

- customising the screens,

- filling fields automatically during data entry with data that is already known to the system.

Periods and Financial Years

Periods and Fiscal Years

A fiscal year (or financial year) corresponds to twelve months for a company. In many countries, the fiscal year corresponds to a calendar year. That may not be the case in other countries.

The financial year can be divided into monthly or three-monthly accounting periods (when you have a quarterly declaration).

OpenERP's management of the fiscal year is flexible enough to enable you to work on several years at the same time. This gives you several advantages, such as the possibility to create three-year budgets.

27.1 Defining a Period or a Financial Year

To define your fiscal year, use the menu *Accounting* → *Configuration* → *Financial Accounting* → *Periods* → *Fiscal Year*. You can create several years in advance to define long-term budgets.

Figure 27.1: *Defining a Financial Year and Periods*

First enter the date of the first day and the last day of your fiscal year. Then, to create the periods, click one of the two buttons at the bottom depending on whether you want to create twelve 1-month or four 3-months periods:

- *Create Monthly Periods* ,
- *Create 3 Months Periods* .

OpenERP automatically creates an opening period to allow you to post your outstanding balances from the previous fiscal year. Notice the `Opening/Closing Period` checkbox for such a period.

27.2 Closing a Period

To close a financial period, for example when a tax declaration has been made, go to the menu *Accounting→ Configuration → Financial Accounting → Periods → Periods*. Click the green arrow to close the period for which you want no more entries to be posted.

Opening Closed Periods

The system administrator can re-open a period should a period have been closed by mistake.

When a period is closed, you can no longer create or modify any transactions in that period. Closing a period is not obligatory, and you could easily leave periods open.

To close an accounting period you can also use the menu *Accounting→ Periodical Processing → End of Period → Close a Period*.

Managing your Tax Structure 28

This section deals with statutory taxes and accounts which are legally required from the company:

- the taxation structure provided by Open ERP,

You can attach taxes to transactions so that you can:

- add taxes to the amount you pay or receive,
- report on the taxes in various categories that you should pay the tax authorities,
- track taxes in your general accounts,
- manage the payment and refund of taxes using the same mechanisms OpenERP uses for other monetary transactions.

Since the detailed tax structure is a mechanism for carrying out governments' policies, and the collection of taxes so critical to their authorities, tax requirements and reporting can be complex. OpenERP has a flexible mechanism for handling taxation that can be configured to meet the requirements of many tax jurisdictions.

The taxation mechanism can also be used to handle other tax-like financial transactions, such as royalties to authors based on the value of transactions through an account.

From the menu *Accounting* → *Configuration* → *Financial Accounting* → *Taxes* you can define your tax structure. Note that when you use a predefined (localised) chart of accounts, taxes will be configured as well in most cases.

OpenERP's tax system runs around three major concepts:

- *Tax Code* (or *Tax Case*), used for tax reporting, can be set up in a hierarchical structure so that multiple codes can be formed into trees in the same way as a `Chart of Accounts`. The Tax Codes structure is used to define your VAT return; it can be numeric and alphanumeric. You can define tax codes from the menu :menuselection: *Accounting –> Configuration –> Financial Accounting –> Taxes –> Tax Codes*.

- *Taxes*, the basic tax object that contains the rules for calculating tax on the transaction it is attached to, linked to the General Accounts and to the Tax Codes. A tax can contain multiple child taxes and base its calculation on those taxes rather than on the base transaction, providing considerable flexibility.

- the *General Accounts*, which record the taxes owing and paid. Since the general accounts are discussed elsewhere in this part of the book and are not tax-specific, they will not be detailed in this section.

You can attach zero or more *Purchase Taxes* and *Sale Taxes* items to products, so that you can account separately for purchase and sales taxes (or Input and Output VAT – where VAT is Value Added Tax).

Because you can attach more than one tax, you can handle a VAT or Sales Tax separately from an Eco Tax on the same product.

To create a new *Tax Code*, use the menu *Accounting → Configuration → Financial Accounting → Taxes → Tax Codes*. You should define the following fields:

Figure 28.1: *Tax Code*

- *Tax Case Name*: a unique name required to identify the tax case, usually taken from your VAT return,

- *Case Code*: an optional short code for the case,

- *Parent Code*: a link to a parent Tax Code to create a tree structure which can be displayed from the menu *Accounting → Charts → Cgart of Taxes*,

- *Not Printable in Invoice*: a checkbox allowing you to indicate that any taxes linked to the tax code concerned should not be printed on the invoice,

- *Coefficient for parent*: choose 1.00 to add the total to the parent account or −1.00 to subtract it,

- *Description*: a free text field for documentation purposes.

You can also see two read-only fields:

- *Period Sum*: a single figure showing the total accumulated on this case for the current financial period.

- *Year Sum*: a single figure showing the total accumulated on this case for the financial year.

You will probably need to create two tax codes for each different tax rate that you have to define, one for the tax itself and one for the invoice amount (the so-called base code) the tax is computed from. And you will create tax codes that you will not link to any tax objects (similar to General Account View types) just to organise the tree (or hierarchical) structure.

To have a look at the structure you have constructed, you can use the menu *Accounting → Charts → Chart of Taxes*. This tree view reflects the structure of the *Tax Codes* and shows the current tax situation for the selected period, or for the complete financial year.

The *Taxes* defined are used to compute taxes on the transactions they are attached to, and they are linked to the corresponding General Accounts (usually VAT accounts) and to Tax Codes, both for the base amount and the tax amount.

To create a new Tax, use the menu *Accounting → Configuration → Financial Accounting → Taxes → Taxes*.

Figure 28.2: *Defining Taxes*

You define the following fields:

- *Tax Name*: a unique name required for this tax (such as 21% Purchase VAT),

- *Tax Code*: an optional code for this tax (such as VAT IN IC),

- *Tax Application*: defines whether the tax is applicable to Sale, Purchase or All transactions,

- *Tax Included in Price*: when checked, the price shown in the product or invoice is inclusive of this tax,

- *Tax Type*: a required field indicating how tax should be calculated: Percentage, Fixed Amount, None, Balance or Python Code, (the latter is found in the *Compute Code* field in the *Special Computation* tab),

- *Amount*: a required field whose meaning depends on the Tax Type, being a multiplier of the base amount when the *Tax Type* is Percentageand a fixed amount added to the base amount when the *Tax Type* is Fixed Amount,

- *Invoice Tax Account*: a General Account used to record invoiced tax amounts, which may be the same for several taxes or split according to percentage so that one tax is allocated to one account,

- *Refund Tax Account*: a General Account used to record invoiced tax refunds, which may be the same as the Invoice Tax Account or, in some tax jurisdictions, has to be separated,

- *Tax on Children*: when checked, the tax calculation is applied to the output from other tax calculations specified in the *Child Tax Accounts* field (so you can have taxes on taxes), otherwise the calculation is applied to the base amount of the transaction,

- *Include in base amount*: when checked, the tax is added to the base amount and not shown separately, such as Eco taxes,

- *Child Tax Accounts*: other taxes that can be used to supply the figure for taxation.

Using Child Taxes

You can use child taxes when you have a complex tax situation requiring several tax codes to be used.

The fields above apply the taxes that you specify and record them in the general accounts, but do not provide you with the information that your tax authorities might need. Use the *Tax Definition* tab, parts Tax Declaration: Invoices and Credit Notes to define to which tax codes the tax should be assigned:

- *Account Base Code*: tax code to record the invoiced amount (exclusive of taxes) the tax is calculated on,

- *Account Tax Code*: tax code to record the calculated tax amount,

- *Refund Base Code*: tax code to record the refund amount (exclusive of taxes) the tax is calculated on,

- *Refund Tax Code*: tax code to record the refund tax amount.

When you have created a tax structure consisting of taxe codes and taxes, you can use the taxes in your various business objects so that transactions can be associated with taxes and tax-like charges, such as Eco Taxes (Recupel and Bebat, for instance).

Retail Customers

When you are retailing to end users rather than selling to a business, you may want to (or be required to) show tax-inclusive prices on your invoicing documents rather than a tax-exclusive price plus tax.

You can assign multiple taxes to a Product. Assuming you have set up the appropriate taxes, you would use the menu *Sales → Products → Products* to open and edit a *Product* definition, then:

- select one or more *Sale Taxes* for any products that you might sell, which may include a `Sales Tax` or `Output VAT` and a `Sales Eco Tax`,

- select one or more *Purchase Taxes* for any products that you might purchase, which may include a `Purchase Tax` or `Input VAT` and a `Purchase Eco Tax`.

Generally, when you make a purchase or sales, the taxes assigned to the product are used to calculate the taxes owing or owed.

You can also assign multiple taxes to an account, so that when you transfer money through the account you attract a tax amount. This principle can easily be used when posting purchase invoices for which no products are required. Taxes on Products and Accounts will usually be national taxes. OpenERP is capable of automatically converting national taxes to intracommunal or export taxes through the concept of `Fiscal Positions`.

Go to the menu *Accounting → Configuration -_> Financial Accounting → Taxes → Fiscal Positions.* You can use the fiscal positions to automatically convert national taxes to the required intracommunal or export taxes, according to the fiscal position specified for the customer or supplier.

Fiscal positions allow you to make a mapping from national taxes to intracommunal or export taxes, or to map your accounts according to these criteria. You can link fiscal positions to your customers and suppliers to ensure automatic and easy VAT conversion when posting entries.

Chart of Accounts

When configuring the software, OpenERP allows you to choose predefined charts of accounts, which include all basic configuration, such as tax codes and fiscal positions. Of course, you can also define your own chart of accounts.

29.1 Using a Preconfigured Chart of Accounts

On installation, the software allows you to select a default chart of accounts from a huge list of predefined charts. To install the chart of accounts as well as the tax definitions for your own country (in most cases), select the chart corresponding to your country from the `Installation Wizard`. The `Generic Chart of Accounts` offers a default (but limited) set of accounts which can be used as a basic chart in any country. The `Chart of Accounts` list also includes a lot of localised charts of accounts.

Figure 29.1: *Starting from a Generic Chart of Accounts*

The wizard will change a bit according to the chart of accounts you select. For the Generic Chart you will be able to add a tax percentage, which will not be the case when you install, for instance, the chart named `Belgium - Plan Comptable Minimum Normalise`. Here OpenERP will automatically install the tax configuration for Belgium too. You will, however, be able to select the default sales and purchase tax to be added when you create a new product.

Figure 29.2: *Starting from a Belgian Chart of Accounts*

Please keep in mind that even when you use a default chart of accounts, you can still modify it to fit your needs.

Modules

You can install a chart from the list of modules too, so simply skip the installation wizard then. The module name will be like `l10n_XX` where XX represents your country code in two letters. For example, to get the chart of accounts for Belgium, go to *Settings → Modules → Modules* and install the module `l10n_be`. This will propose the exact same chart from the wizard (`Belgium - Plan Comptable Minimum Normalise`).

Some of these pre-defined charts of accounts are comprehensive and accurate, others rather have a more tentative status and are simply indicators of the possibilities. You can modify these, or build your own accounts onto the default chart, or replace it entirely with a custom chart.

29.2 Creating a Chart of Accounts

Start by creating *Account Types*, which determine the kind of account and the way in which accounts will be treated at financial year closing.

To add, modify or delete existing account types, go to the menu *Accounting → Configuration → Financial Accounting → Accounts → Account Types*.

Figure 29.3: *Defining Account Types*

The fields used to define an account type are the following:

- *Account Type*: the name of the account type.

- *Code*: the code of the account type.

- *PL/BS Category*: this category determines where in a report the account will be printed (i.e. Balance Sheet and Profit and Loss). There are five types you can use: No type at all (/), Balance Sheet (Assets Accounts = active), Balance Sheet (Liabilities Accounts = passive), Profit & Loss (Income) and Profit & Loss (Expense).

- *Deferral Method*: this field indicates how and whether the account will be transferred at financial year closing.

  - None means that the account will not be transferred. Typically used for profit and loss accounts.

- Balance means that the account balance will be transferred at year closing. Typically used for balance sheet accounts.

- Detail means that every single entry will be transferred to the next financial year.

- Unreconciled means that only unreconciled (outstanding) entries will be transferred to the next financial year. Typically used for centralisation accounts.

- *Sign on Reports*: this field allows you to reverse the sign of accounts, such as Income accounts being printed positive instead of the default negative. Use Reverse balance sign to accomplish this.

Use the *View* type for accounts that make up the structure of the charts and have no account data inputs of their own.

To add, modify or delete existing accounts, use the menu *Accounting → Configuration → Financial Accounting → Accounts → Accounts*.

Figure 29.4: *Defining Accounts*

The main account fields are:

- *Name*: the account name.

- *Code*: the code length is not limited to a specific number of digits. Use code 0 to indicate the root account.

- *Parent*: determines which account is the parent of this one, to create the tree structure of the chart of accounts.

- *Internal Type*: internal types have special effects in OpenERP. By default, the following types are available: View can be used to create a hierarchical structure for your accounts (grouping), Regular any account that does not fit into one of the other types; most of the accounts will have this type, Receivable - Payable: these types are used to indicate the centralisation accounts (for customers and suppliers) that will be set for each partner, Liquidity used to indicate financial accounts (bank and cash accounts), Consolidation to create a virtual (or consolidation) chart of accounts, Closed to indicate accounts that are no longer used.

- *Account Type*: it is important to select the corresponding account type, as explained above. This will have an impact at year closing and also when printing reports.

- *Secondary Currency*: forces all the moves for this account to have this secondary currency. Note that you can also define exchange rates from the menu *Accounting → Configuration → Miscellaneous → Currencies*.

- *Outgoing Currencies Rate*: to be selected only when you add a secondary currency. You have two options for outgoing transactions: `At Date` or `Average Rate`. Incoming transactions are always calculated `At Date`, according to the date of the transaction.

- *Allow Reconciliation*: determines if you can reconcile the entries in this account. Activate this field for receivable and payable accounts and any other account that need to be reconciled other than by bank statements.

- *Default Taxes*: this is the default tax applied to purchases or sales using this account. It enables the system to propose tax entries automatically when entering data in a journal manually.

The tree structure of the accounts can be altered as often and as much as you wish without recalculating any of the individual entries. So you can easily restructure your account during the year to reflect the reality of the company better.

You can have a look at active charts of accounts using the menu *Accounting → Charts → Chart of Accounts*, and *Open Charts* for the selected year, account moves and periods. Click an account to drill down to its details.

Hierarchical Charts

Most accounting software packages represent their charts of accounts in the form of a list. You can do this in OpenERP as well if you want to, but its tree view offers several advantages:

- it lets you show in detail only the accounts that interest you,

- it enables you to get a global view of accounts (when you show only summary accounts),

- it is more intuitive, because you can search for accounts on the basis of their classification,

- it is flexible because you can easily restructure them.

The structure of the chart of accounts is hierarchical, with account subtotals calculated from the `View` accounts. You can develop a set of view accounts to contain only those elements that interest you.

To get the details of the account entries that are important to you, all you need to do is click the account's code or name.

Displaying the chart of accounts can take several seconds, because OpenERP calculates the debits, credits and balance for each account in real time.

29.3 Virtual Charts of Accounts

The structure of a chart of accounts is imposed by the legislation in effect in the country concerned. Unfortunately, that structure does not always correspond to the view that a company needs.

In OpenERP, you can use the concept of virtual charts of accounts to manage several representations of the same accounts simultaneously. These representations can be shown in real time with no additional data entry.

So your general chart of accounts can be the one imposed by the statutes of your country, and your CEO can then have other virtual charts as necessary, based on the accounts in the general chart. For example, you can create a view per department, a cash-flow and liquidity view, or consolidated accounts for different companies.

The most interesting thing about virtual charts of accounts is that they can be used in the same way as the default chart of accounts for the whole organization. For example, you can establish budgets from your consolidated accounts or from the accounts from one of your companies.

Virtual Accounts

Virtual accounts enable you to provide different representations of one or several existing charts of accounts. Creating and restructuring virtual accounts has no impact on the accounting entries. You can then use the virtual charts with no risk of altering the general chart of accounts or future accounting entries.

Because they are used only to get a different representation of the same entries, they are very useful for:

- consolidating several companies in real time,

- reporting to a holding according to their chart of accounts,

- depreciation calculations,

- cash-flow views,

- getting more useful views than those imposed,

- presenting summary charts to other users that are appropriate to their general system rights.

So there are good reasons for viewing the impact of financial transactions through virtual charts, such as budgets and financial indicators based on special views of the company.

To create a new chart of accounts you should create a root account using the menu *Accounting → Configuration → Financial Accounting → Accounts → Accounts*. Your top level account should have a name, a code (different from any other code in your current chart), an *Internal Type* and *Account Type* View. Then you can choose your structure by creating other accounts of *Account Type* Views as necessary. The *Internal Type* should be of the `Consolidation` type if you want to map accounts. Check your virtual structure using the menu *Financial Management → Charts → Charts of Accounts* and select the corresponding chart in the drop-down list at the top of the screen.

To be able to map your virtual chart of accounts to your general chart of accounts, you have to set *Internal Type* as `Consolidation`. From the *Consolidated Children* you can then map accounts or make accounts consolidate. In the *Consolidated Children*, you can add `View` accounts or normal accounts. If you add a `View` account to the consolidated children, OpenERP will automatically include all existing and future linked accounts.

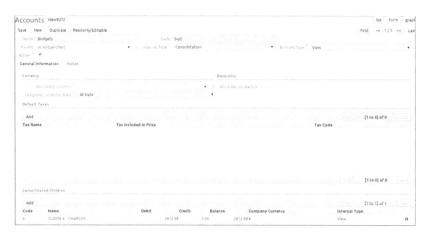

Figure 29.5: *Virtual Accounts Mapped to View Account*

You can then run reports such as *Trial Balance* and *General Ledger* for both your general chart of accounts and your virtual chart(s) giving you another representation of the company. All the actions and states in your general account are also available in the virtual accounts.

Finally, you can also make virtual charts of accounts from other virtual charts. That can give an additional dimension for financial analysis. You can create an unlimited number of virtual (consolidation) charts of accounts.

Journals 30

All your accounting entries need to appear in an accounting journal. So you should create a Sales Journal for customer invoices, a Sales Refund journal for customer credit notes, a Purchase Journal for supplier invoices, a Purchase Refund journal for supplier credit notes and a Bank Journal for bank transactions.

30.1 Configuring a Journal

To view, edit or create new journals use the menu *Accounting → Configuration → Financial Accounting → Journals → Journals*.

Figure 30.1: *Defining an Accounting Journal*

Blue fields are mandatory fields. When you select a journal type, some configuration parameters will be preset. The journal type will tell the system where the journal concerned can be used.

Each journal has a specific way of displaying data. The type of journal determines the journal view, which indicates the fields that need to be visible and are required to enter accounting data in that journal. The view determines both the order of the fields and the properties of each field. For example, the field *Statement* has to appear when entering data in the bank journal, but not in the other journals.

You can also create your own journal views. However, before creating a new view for a journal, check whether there is nothing similar already defined. You should only create a new view for new types of journals.

You can create a sequence for each journal. This sequence determines the automatic numbering for accounting entries. Several journals can use the same sequence if you want to define one for them all, and if your legislation allows this.

Sequences

Sequences can also be created from the *Settings → Configuration → Sequences & Identifiers → Sequences*. By default, OpenERP has only one sequence in the journal definition. If you need two separate sequences to be kept for the journal, you can install the module `account_sequence`.

The default credit and debit account allow the software to automatically generate counterpart entries when you are entering data through *Journal Items*. In some journals, debit and credit accounts are mandatory. For example, in a bank journal you should put an associated bank account, so that you do not have to create counterparts for each transaction manually.

A journal can be marked as being centralised. When you do this, the counterpart entries will not be owned by each entry, but will be global for the given journal and period. You will then have a credit line and a debit line centralized for each entry in one of these journals, meaning that both credit and debit appear on the same line. This option is used when posting opening entries in a situation journal.

> **Bank Journal, Easy Configuration**
>
> A bank journal can automatically be created from the bank account(s) you define for your company. Go to *Accounting → Configuration → Financial Accounting → Accounts → Setup your Bank Accounts*. Here you create the bank account or IBAN number of your company's bank account(s). Fill in the Bank Name, and when you save the entry, your Bank Journal will automatically be created with the Bank Name and the Account Number. The general ledger account for this bank will also be created for you.

30.2 Controls and Tips for Data Entry

You can carry out two types of control on journals in OpenERP – controls over the accounts and access controls for groups of users. In addition to these controls, you can also apply all of the standard user rights management.

To avoid entering account data in wrong accounts, you can put conditions on the general accounts about which journal can use a given account. To do this, you have to list all the accounts or valid account types in the second tab, *Entry Controls*. If you have not added any accounts there, OpenERP applies no restriction on the accounts for that journal. If you list accounts and/or the types of accounts that can be used in a journal, OpenERP prevents you from using any account or account type not in that list. This verification step starts from the moment you enter data. You can only select allowed accounts or account types.

This functionality is useful for limiting possible data entry errors by restricting the accounts to be used in a journal.

Control of Data Entry

In accounting it is not a good idea to allow a data entry directly from bank account A to bank account B. If you enter a transaction from bank A to bank B, the transaction will be accounted for twice.

To prevent this problem, pass the transaction through intermediate account C. At the time of data entry, the system checks the type of account that is accepted in the bank journal: only accounts that are not of type `Bank` are accepted.

If your accountant defines this control properly, non-accounting users are prevented from transferring payments from one bank to another, reducing your risks.

Payment Terms 31

You can define whatever payment terms you need in OpenERP. Payment terms determine the due dates for paying an invoice.

To define new payment terms, use the menu *Accounting → Configuration → Miscellaneous → Payment Terms* and then click *New*.

The figure below represents the following payment term: 5000 within 5 days, 50% payment at the last day of current month, Remaining on 15th of next month.

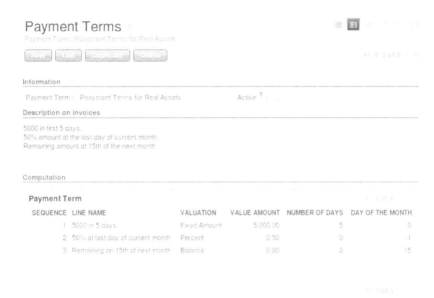

Figure 31.1: *Configuring payment terms*

To configure new conditions, start by giving a name to the *Payment Term* field. Text that you put in the field *Description on invoices*, is used on invoices, so enter a clear description of the payment terms there.

Then create individual lines for calculating the terms in the section *Payment Term*. You must give each line a name (*Line Name*). These give an informative title and do not affect the actual calculation of terms. The *Sequence* field lets you define the order in which the rules are evaluated.

The *Valuation* field enables you to calculate the amount to pay for each line:

- Percent : the line corresponds to a percentage of the total amount, the factor being given in *Value Amount*. The number indicated in *Value Amount* must take a value between 0 and 1.

- Fixed Amount : this is a fixed value given by the *Value Amount* box.

- Balance : indicates the balance remaining after accounting for the other lines.

Think carefully about setting the last line of the calculation to `Balance`, to avoid rounding errors. The highest sequence number is evaluated last.

The two last fields, *Number of Days* and *Day of the Month*, enable the calculation of the delay in payment for each line. The delay *Day of the Month* can be set to -1, 0 or any positive number. For example, if today is 20th December 2010, and if you want to set payment terms like this:

- *5000 within 5 days*: set *Valuation* `Fixed Amount`, *Number of Days* 5 and *Day of the Month* 0. That creates journal entry for date 25th December 2010.

- *50% payment at the last day of current month*: set *Valuation* `Percent`, *Number of Days* 0 and *Day of the Month* -1. That creates journal entry for date 31st December 2010.

- *Remaining on 15th of next month*: set *Valuation* `Balance`, *Number of Days* 0 and *Day of the Month* 15. That creates journal entry for date 15th January 2011.

You can then add payment terms to a Partner through the tab *Accounting* on the partner form.

Opening and Closing a Financial Year   32

At the end of a financial year, you will have to transfer the closing balance of that year as an opening balance to the new financial year. OpenERP allows you to automatically post such an entry. You can transfer the new opening balance numerous times, because it is impossible to close a year at once. Correction entries will have to be made, due to which balances will change. The new balance can easily be transferred through a wizard, so you do not have to keep track of each correction entry made in the previous financial year.

> **OpenERP Accounting**
>
> The procedure below is valid if you already have a financial year with entries in OpenERP.

32.1 Steps to Open a New Financial Year in an Existing OpenERP Configuration

Before generating the opening balance for your various accounts, you have to go through several steps.

1. Create the new Financial Year

Create the new financial year as explained in *Defining a Period or a Financial Year* (page 129).

2. Define an Opening Period

Go to *Accounting → Configuration → Financial Accounting → Periods → Periods* and create a new period for the financial year you wish to open (in case it has not been generated automatically). Make sure to link the period to the newly defined financial year. Select the *Opening/Closing Period* checkbox to indicate that this period should be used for opening entries. Both dates typically match the first day of your financial year (e.g. 01/01/YYYY).

3. Check the Account Types

Before generating the opening entries, make sure to check the defined account types, more specifically the *Deferral Method*. The deferral method determines whether and how account entries will be transferred to the new financial year. There are four possible deferral methods: None, Balance, Detail, Unreconciled.

Deferral Method	Action
None	Nothing will be transferred (typically P&L accounts)
Balance	Account balance will be transferred (typically Balance Sheet accounts)
Detail	All entries are transferred, also reconciled entries
Unreconciled	Only entries that are not reconciled on the first day of the new financial year will be transferred (typically receivable and payable)

4. Check the Link between Account and Account Type.

Check whether each account is linked to the correct account type to avoid generating an incorrect opening entry.

5. Create an Opening/Closing Journal

Go to *Accounting → Configuration → Financial Accounting → Journals → Journals*. Create a new journal to post your opening entries. Make sure to respect the following settings:

1. *Type* should be *Opening/Closing Situation*.

2. *Standard debit/credit account* could be something like 140000 Benefits.

3. *Centralised counterpart* will be checked automatically when select the journal type, to avoid a counterpart on each line, and instead have one debit and one credit entry on the corresponding opening account.

4. The *Entry Sequence* will also be created automatically on save.

32.2 Generating the Opening Entry

To automatically generate the opening entries based on your actual books, OpenERP provides a wizard. Go to *Accounting → Periodical Processing → End of Period → Generate Opening Entries*.

In the wizard, enter the financial year for which you want to transfer the balances (*Fiscal Year to close*). Select the *New Fiscal Year* (the year in which you want to generate the opening entry). You also have to select the journal and the period to post the opening entries. The description for the opening entry is proposed by default, but of course you can enter your own description, such as *Opening Entry for financial year YYYY*. Then you click the *Create* button to generate the opening entry according to the settings defined.

To have a look at the draft opening entry that has been generated, go to *Accounting → Journal Entries → Journal Entries*. Click the *Unposted* button to filter only draft entries. Open the corresponding entry and verify the data. Click the *Post* button to confirm the entry.

Changes in Previous Financial Year

As long as the audit is ongoing, extra entries may be added to the financial year to close. To automatically have the correct balances, OpenERP allows you to use the *Cancel Opening Entries* wizard. This wizard will automatically cancel the existing opening entry.

To update the balances to show the correct results, you should run the *Generate Opening Entries:guilabel:* wizard again. The new opening entry will contain the correct balances. This way, you can generate your opening entry as many times as required.

32.3 Closing a Financial Year

To close a financial year, use the menu *Accounting→ Periodical Processing → End of Period → Close a Fiscal Year*. A wizard opens asking you for the financial year to close.

When the year is closed, you can no longer create or modify any transactions in that year. So you should always make a backup of the database before closing the fiscal year. Closing a year is not mandatory, and you could easily do that sometime in the following year, when your accounts are finally sent to the statutory authorities, and no further modifications are permitted.

Figure 32.1: *Closing a Financial Year*

Steps to Start your Financial Year   33

When you decide to do your accounting in OpenERP, and you already have an accounting system, you should enter your opening balance and outstanding entries in OpenERP. Make sure you configure your accounting system as explained in the Configuration chapter. Below we explain the minimal configuration required to post your opening balance and outstanding entries.

1. Create the new Financial Year

Create the new financial year as explained in *Defining a Period or a Financial Year* (page 129).

2. Define an Opening Period

Go to *Accounting → Configuration → Financial Accounting → Periods → Periods* and create a new period for the financial year you wish to open (in case it has not been generated automatically). Make sure to link the period to the newly defined financial year. Select the *Opening/Closing Period* checkbox to indicate that this period should be used for opening entries. Both dates typically match the first day of your financial year (e.g. 01/01/YYYY).

3. Check the Account Types

Before generating the opening entries, make sure to check the defined account types, more specifically the *Deferral Method*. The deferral method determines whether and how account entries will be transferred to the new financial year. There are four possible deferral methods: None, Balance, Detail, Unreconciled.

Deferral Method	Action
None	Nothing will be transferred (typically P&L accounts)
Balance	Account balance will be transferred (typically Balance Sheet accounts)
Detail	All entries are transferred, also reconciled entries
Unreconciled	Only entries that are not reconciled on the first day of the new financial year will be transferred (typically receivable and payable)

4. Define Accounts

Check whether each account with an opening balance has been defined in the Chart of Accounts and is linked to the correct account type. We recommend you to define one or more suspense accounts to post your outstanding entries from the previous financial year. Check the *Reconcile* for such suspense accounts, because their balance will be zero.

5. Create an Opening/Closing Journal

Go to *Accounting → Configuration → Financial Accounting → Journals → Journals*. Create a new journal to post your opening entries. Make sure to respect the following settings:

1. *Type* should be *Opening/Closing Situation*.

2. *Standard debit/credit account* could be something like 140000 Benefits.

3. *Centralised counterpart* will be checked automatically when select the journal type, to avoid a counterpart on each line, and instead have one debit and one credit entry on the corresponding opening account.

4. The *Entry Sequence* will also be created automatically on save.

6. Create a Purchase and/or Sales Journal for Outstanding Entries

We recommend you to create separate purchase and sales journals to post the outstanding entries from your previous accounting system. This will allow you to easily keep track of your opening entries.

Go to *Accounting → Configuration → Financial Accounting → Journals → Journals*. Create a new purchase and sales journal to post your outstanding entries. Make sure to respect the following settings:

1. *Type* should be *Purchase* or *Sales*.

2. The *Entry Sequence* will also be created automatically on save.

Now you can start entering your outstanding customer and supplier entries according to your list of open entries at the end of the year.

Go to the menu *Accounting → Customers → Customer Invoices* to post your outstanding sales entries. To post your outstanding purchase entries, go to Go to the menu *Accounting → Suppliers → Supplier Invoices*.

We recommend you to use suspense accounts instead of expense or income accounts. Indeed, your expense and income accounts have already been posted in the previous financial year, and there is no need to transfer these balances. The outstanding entries from previous financial years should not contain any VAT entries; they only get the balance the customer still has to pay you, or the balance you have to pay to the supplier.

7. Enter the Opening Balance (Miscellaneous Entry)

For each account that needs to be reopened, enter account data (debit or credit) in the journal. For this operation, go to the menu *Accounting → Journal Entries → Journal Entries* and select a miscellaneous journal.

Import

You can also use OpenERP's generic import tool if you load the balance of each of your accounts from other accounting software.

Putting Analytic Accounts in Place   34

For the initial setup of good analytic accounts you should:

- set up the chart of accounts,

- create the different journals,

- link the analytic journals to your accounting journals.

34.1 Setting up the Chart of Accounts

Start by choosing the most suitable analytic representation for your company before entering it into
OpenERP. To create the different analytic accounts, use the menu *Accounting→ Configuration →
Analytic Accounting → Analytic Accounts* and click the *Create* button. Note that the data you see
when creating an analytic account will depend upon the business applications installed.

Figure 34.1: *Setting up an Analytic Account*

To create an analytic account, you have to complete the main fields:

- the *Account Name*,

- the *Code/Reference*: used as a shortcut for selecting the account,

- the *Parent Analytic Account*: use this field to define the hierarchy between the accounts.

- the *Account Type*: just like general accounts, the `View` type is used for virtual accounts which are
  used only to create a hierarchical structure and for subtotals, and not to store accounting entries.
  The `Normal` type will be used for analytic accounts containing entries.

If an analytic account (e.g. a project) is for a limited time, you can define a start and end date here.

The *Maximum Time* can be used for contracts with a fixed limit of hours to use.

Invoicing

You have several methods available to you in OpenERP for automated invoicing:

- Service companies usually use invoicing from purchase orders, analytic accounts or project management tasks.

- Manufacturing and trading companies more often use invoicing from deliveries or customer purchase orders.

For more information about invoicing from projects, we refer to the book (soon to be released) about Project and Services Management.

Once you have defined the different analytic accounts, you can view your chart through the menu *Accounting → Charts → Chart of Analytic Accounts*. You can display analytic accounts for one or more periods or for an entire financial year.

Figure 34.2: *Analytic Chart of Accounts*

Setting up an Analytic Account

The setup screen for an analytic account can vary according to the modules installed in your database. For example, you will see information about recharging services only if you have the module `hr_timesheet_invoice` installed.

Some of these modules add helpful management statistics to the analytic account. The most useful is probably the module `account_analytic_analysis`, which adds such information as indicators about your margins, invoicing amounts, and latest service dates and invoice dates.

34.2 Creating Journals

Once the analytic chart has been created for your company, you have to create the different journals. These journals enable you to categorise the different accounting entries by their type, such as:

- services,
- expense reimbursements,
- purchases of materials,
- miscellaneous expenditure,
- sales.

Minimal Journals

At a minimum, you have to create one analytic journal for Sales and one for Purchases. If you do not create these two, OpenERP will not validate invoices linked to an analytic account, because it would not be able to create an analytic accounting entry automatically.

Figure 34.3: *Creating an Analytic Journal*

To define your analytic journals, use the menu *Accounting* → *Configuration* → *Analytic Accounting* → *Analytic Journals* then click the *Create* button.

It is easy to create an analytic journal. Just give it a *Journal Name*, a *Journal Code* and a *Type*. The types available are:

- `Sale`, for sales to customers and for credit notes,
- `Purchase`, for purchases and expenses,
- `Cash`, for financial entries,
- `Situation`, to adjust accounts when starting an activity, or at the end of the financial year,
- `General`, for all other entries.

The analytic journal now has to be linked to your general journals to allow OpenERP to post the analytic entries. For example, if you enter an invoice for a customer, OpenERP will automatically search for the analytic journal of type `Sales` linked to your Sales Journal. Go to *Accounting*→ *Configuration* → *Financial Accounting* → *Journals* → *Journals* and select for instance the Sales journal. In the *Analytic Journal* select the analytic sales journal.

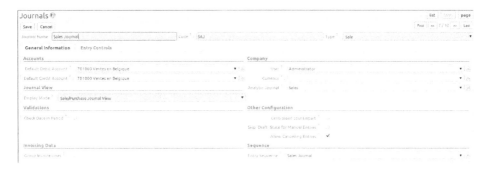

Figure 34.4: *Linking an Analytic Journal to a Journal*

34.3 Working with Analytic Defaults

You can work with analytic default accounts in OpenERP by installing the `account_analytic_default` module. Notice that this module is also linked with the `sale`, `stock` and `procurement` modules.

The system will automatically select analytic accounts according to the following criteria:

- Product

- Partner

- User

- Company

- Date

You can configure these criteria using the menu *Accounting → Configuration → Analytic Accounting → Analytic Defaults* and clicking the *Create* button. According to the criteria you define here, the correct analytic account will be proposed when creating an order or an invoice.

Figure 34.5: *Specify Criteria to Automatically Select Analytic Account*

About the authors

Fabien Pinckaers

Fabien Pinckaers was only eighteen years old when he started his first company. Today, over ten years later, he has founded and managed several new technology companies, all based on Free / Open Source software.

He originated Tiny ERP, now OpenERP, and is the director of two companies including OpenERP S.A., the editor of OpenERP. In a few years time, he has grown the Tiny group from one to sixty-five employees without loans or external fund-raising, and while making a profit.

He has also developed several large scale projects, such as Auction-in-Europe.com, which became the leader in the art market in Belgium. Even today people sell more art works there than on ebay.be.

He is also the founder of the LUG (Linux User Group) of Louvain-la-Neuve, and of several free projects like OpenReport, OpenStuff and Tiny Report. Educated as a civil engineer (polytechnic), he has won several IT prizes in Europe such as Wired and l'Inscene.

A fierce defender of free software in the enterprise, he is in constant demand as a conference speaker and he is the author of numerous articles dealing with free software in the management of the enterprise.

Follow Fabien on his blog http://fptiny.blogspot.com/ or on twitter fpopenerp.

Els Van Vossel

Els Van Vossel always had a dedication to both written and spoken word. Clear and explicit communication is crucial.

Educated as a Professional Translator in Antwerp, she worked as an independent translator on the localization of major ERP software. Els acquired ERP knowledge and decided to start working as a functional ERP consultant and a Technical Communicator for ERP software.

As such, the world of OpenSource software became more and more attractive. She started working with OpenERP software in her free time and doing so, Els really wanted to meet Fabien Pinckaers to share thoughts about documentation and training strategy. Now Els is reviewing and writing OpenERP Books.

Being an author of several Software Manuals, she finds it exciting to work on the OpenERP documentation and continuously take it to a higher level. Please note that this is a hell of a job, but Els finds great pleasure in doing it!

Follow Els on her blog http://training-openerp.blogspot.com/ or on twitter elsvanvossel.

Index

A

absences, 73
account
    type, 138
accounting, 28
    analytical, 28
    auxiliary, 28
    bank statement, 47
    budgetary, 28
    dashboard, 19
    entry, 45
    financial, 28
    invoicing, 51
    multi-company, 28
    workflow, 51
Accounting Management, 25
accounts
    chart, 135
    due date, 42
    start of year, 149
adjustment, 49
    limit, 67
allocation
    cost, 71, 76, 80
analytic
    accounts, 154
    balance, 101
    chart of accounts, 70
    cost ledger, 101
    entries, 80
    records, 77
Analytic Accounts, 67
asset, 28
Asset Management, 116
Assets, 116

B

balance
    aged, 19
    analytic, 101
balance sheet, 86

bank

bank
    statement, 47
budget revisions, 95
budgeting, 94

C

cash management, 49
chart of accounts, 135
    analytic, 70
    virtual, 140
configuration
    setup, 1
Configuring Accounts, 125
consolidation (accounting), 140
cost
    allocation, 71, 76, 80
cost ledger
    analytic, 101
credit note, 31
Credit Notes, 42
creditor, 17
Currency, 104

D

dashboard
    accounting, 19
debtor, 17
declarations, 41
DEEE tax, 38
due date
    accounts, 42

E

entry
    accounting, 45

F

field
    properties, 34
Financial Analysis, 82
financial reporting, 82

fiscal position, 43, 134
fiscal year, 129
follow-up, 22

G

general ledger, 83

I

Initial Setup, 1
Installation, 1
invoice layout, 37
invoices, 32
invoicing, 51, 155
Invoicing & Payments, 7

J

journal, 87
    configuring, 142
    minimal journals, 157

L

ledger, 20
liability, 28

M

module
    account, 28
    account_analytic_analysis, 156
    account_followup, 22
    account_invoice_layout, 37
    account_payment, 63
    account_tax_include, 36
    board_account, 19, 99
    hr_timesheet_invoice, 156
modules
    l10n_, 137
    l10n_be, 137
multi-company, 103
    accounting, 28
Multicurrency, 104

N

navigating relationships, 34

O

OpenERP Online, 3
overdue payments, 22

P

payable, 17
payment terms, 43, 145
payments, 61
period, 129
profit & loss, 86
properties
    field, 34

R

receivable, 17
reconciliation, 54
    manual, 55
reminder, 22
right-click, 34

S

setup, 1
    configuration, 1
statement
    bank, 47
Supplier Payment, 16

T

tax, 131
taxation, 82
trial balance, 83
type
    account, 138

V

VAT, 91
virtual
    chart of accounts, 140